Errata for *Asian Equity Investing*

The following figure replaces Figure 2 on page 55 in Donald Krueger's presentation, which has errors in the equations.

Figure 2. Determining Fair Market Value

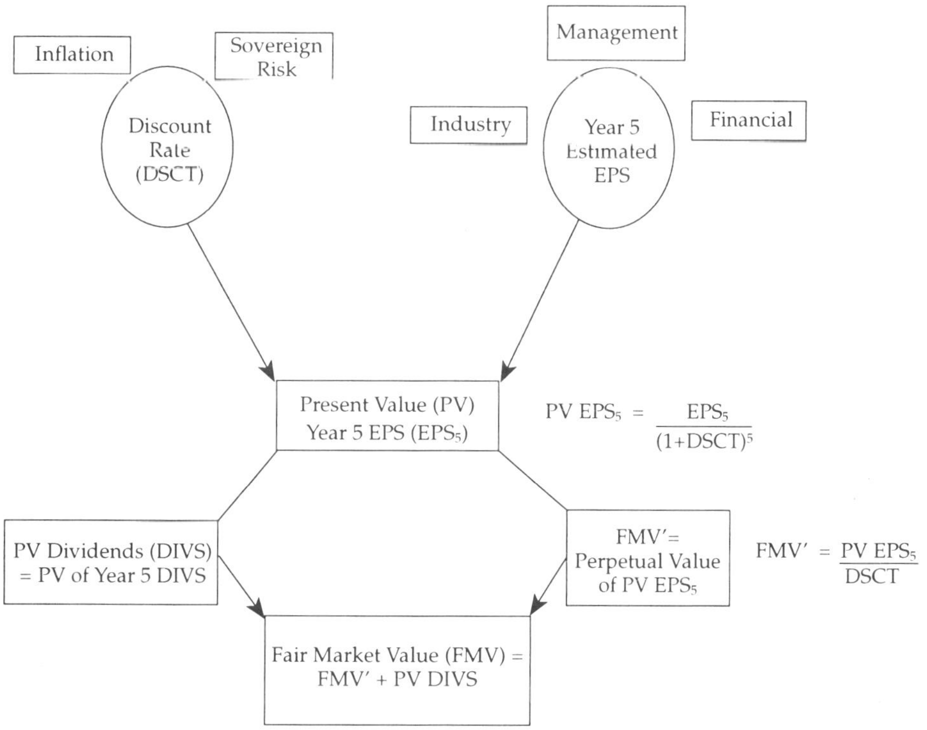

Inflation

Sovereign Risk

Discount Rate (DSCT)

Management

Industry

Year 5 Estimated EPS

Financial

Present Value (PV) Year 5 EPS (EPS_5)

$$\text{PV } EPS_5 = \frac{EPS_5}{(1+DSCT)^5}$$

PV Dividends (DIVS) = PV of Year 5 DIVS

FMV′= Perpetual Value of PV EPS_5

$$FMV' = \frac{\text{PV } EPS_5}{DSCT}$$

Fair Market Value (FMV) = FMV′ + PV DIVS

Note: FMV′ assumes level growth in EPS after Year 5.

ICFA Continuing Education
Asian Equity Investing

Proceedings of the AIMR seminar *Advances in Asian Equity Management: Style Investing*

October 28–29, 1997
Singapore

Richard Bernstein
Ian Burden
Michael Clancy
John K. Koeneman, CFA, *Moderator*
Donald M. Krueger, CFA
Henry D.C. Lee
Letitia Li
Eng Hai Lim
S. Beng Neoh
Shane H. Norman
David S. Roche, CFA
Robert J. Schwob
Robert A. Shakotko
Nigel Tupper
Michael C.M. Wilson
Robert G. Zielinski, CFA

To obtain the *AIMR Publications Catalog*, contact:
AIMR, P.O. Box 3668, Charlottesville, Virginia 22903, U.S.A.
Phone 804-980-3668; Fax 804-980-9755; E-mail info@aimr.org
or
visit AIMR's World Wide Web site at **www.aimr.org**
to view the AIMR publications list.

ICFA Continuing Education is published monthly seven times a year in May, May, May, June, July, August, and September by the Association for Investment Management and Research, P.O. Box 3668, Charlottesville, Virginia 22903, U.S.A. This publication is designed to provide accurate and authoritative information with regard to the subject matter covered. It is sold with the understanding that the publisher is not engaged in rendering legal, accounting, or other professional services. If legal advice or other expert assistance is required, the services of a competent professional should be sought. Periodicals postage paid at the post office in Richmond, Virginia, and additional mailing offices.

Copies are mailed as a benefit of membership to CFA® charterholders. Subscriptions also are available at US$100 for one year. Address all circulation communications to ICFA Continuing Education, P.O. Box 3668, Charlottesville, Virginia 22903, U.S.A.; Phone 804-980-3668; Fax 804-980-9755. For change of address, send mailing label and new address six weeks in advance.

Postmaster: Send address changes to the Association for Investment Management and Research, P.O. Box 3668, Charlottesville, Virginia 22903.

ISBN 0-935015-20-5
Printed in the United States of America
May 1998

Contents

ICFA Board of Trustees, 1997–98

AIMR Education Committee, 1997–98

AIMR Senior Education Staff

Foreword

One might say that Asian investing dates back to the 13th century, when Marco Polo made his famous journeys to China and brought the riches of the East back to Europe. Because Marco Polo realized great wealth from the "investment" he made in time and travel expenses, others soon followed his lead, and the great trade routes were established. The parallel to the 20th century—investors following the lead of others seeking higher returns in Asian markets—is evident. One might even go so far to say that the trials and tribulations that investors face today in Asian equity markets parallel those faced by the 13th century "investors."

Asian equity markets can be tricky places to invest, but the authors of this proceedings offer readers invaluable insight into the market analysis, research techniques, and investment approaches that have proven effective for them. The key message delivered by all these authors is one that may seem obvious but is often overlooked by investors: Asian markets are not U.S. markets. Asian markets need to be analyzed in the context of global and local economics. Companies must be investigated based on local market, regulatory, and cultural considerations. Style approaches to investing (such as value or growth) cannot be applied in the same manner in Asia that they are in the United States. The investment decision-making process should be based on fundamental criteria, in general, but those criteria must take into account local factors, such as liquidity and currency risk.

This proceedings is based on AIMR's "Advances in Asian Equity Management: Style Investing" conference that took place October 28–29, 1997, in Singapore, and perhaps the heightened activity of the Asian markets at that time contributed to the heightened energy that the authors brought to their presentations.

We are grateful to John K. Koeneman, CFA, for his fine work as moderator of the seminar. We would also like to extend our gratitude to the Singapore Society of Financial Analysts for hosting the seminar. The authors of this proceedings devoted considerable time and effort to discussing the complexities of Asian equity investing and are well deserving of our thanks: Richard Bernstein, Merrill Lynch & Company; Donald M. Krueger, CFA, Valenzuela Capital Partners, Inc.; David S. Roche, CFA, Independent Strategy, Ltd.; Robert J. Schwob, Style Investment Research Associates Limited; Nigel Tupper, Merrill Lynch & Company, Singapore; Michael C.M. Wilson, J.P. Morgan & Company, Inc.; and Robert G. Zielinski, CFA, Jardine Fleming Securities, Limited, Singapore.

Although investing in Asian markets may not be a new phenomenon, investors are always looking for new investment approaches and an increased understanding of the region's markets. Such insight can certainly be gained from this proceedings.

Katrina F. Sherrerd, CFA
Senior Vice President
Educational Products

Biographies

Richard Bernstein is first vice president and director of quantitative and equity derivatives research at Merrill Lynch & Company. Prior to joining Merrill Lynch, he was an investment strategist/quantitative analyst at E.F. Hutton and also at Tucker Anthony & R.L. Day. Mr. Bernstein serves on the board of directors of the Society of Quantitative Analysts. He has been selected for *Institutional Investor*'s All-America Research Team in the categories of quantitative analysis and equity derivatives. Mr. Bernstein holds an A.B. in economics from Hamilton College and an M.B.A. in finance from New York University.

John K. Koeneman, CFA, founder, managing director, and chief investment officer of Koeneman Capital Management, leads KCM's portfolio management team in setting investment policy, strategy, and asset allocation. Before founding KCM, he managed Singapore's foreign reserves as consultant and director of equities for the Government of Singapore Investment Corporation. Previously, Mr. Koeneman was employed by State Street Bank, where he helped develop the first international index fund. Mr. Koeneman earned a B.S. in metallurgy from the Massachusetts Institute of Technology and an M.B.A. from Harvard Business School.

Donald M. Krueger, CFA, is a managing director of Valenzuela Capital Partners, Inc., where he established and manages Pan Asia Fund, Ltd., a hedge fund that invests in Asia ex-Japan securities. He previously held the positions of managing director at Soros Fund Management and vice president at Templeton International. In addition, Mr. Krueger conducted global research and managed assets at Capital Research Company. In 1986, he was named one of the top 10 buy-side analysts by *Institutional Investor.* He holds a B.A. in economics from the University of Rochester and an M.B.A. from Harvard Business School.

David S. Roche, CFA, is president and global strategist at Independent Strategy, Ltd., in London. He is a frequent contributor to the *Wall Street Journal* and a regular commentator on the BBC, CNN, and CNBC television networks. Previously, Mr. Roche was managing director, head of research, and global strategist at Morgan Stanley. Before joining Morgan Stanley, he was a senior fund manager and asset allocator at J.P. Morgan Investment Management. Mr. Roche holds an M.A. from Trinity College, Dublin, and an M.B.A. from INSEAD.

Robert J. Schwob is the founding chief executive of Style Investment Research Associates Limited, a style advisory service provider offering international investors style advice, analysis, and analytical support. He is also a director of INQUIRE (UK) and chairman of the INQUIRE (UK) Research Committee. Mr. Schwob was formerly chief executive of Quorum Capital Management in London and chief investment officer for the Citibank Private Bank (Europe, Middle East, and Africa). He holds masters' degrees in mathematics and international economics.

Nigel Tupper is vice president and quantitative analyst for the Asia Pacific region for Merrill Lynch & Company, Singapore. Previously, Mr. Tupper held the position of investment manager with Credit Suisse First Boston Investment Management, Australia, where he was responsible for the development of quantitative models to enhance security products. Prior to this work, he served with Bankers Trust Australia. The Greenwich Fund Manager Survey recently ranked him first for quantitative research for the Asia Pacific Region. Mr. Tupper received bachelor of economics and bachelor of science degrees from the Australian National University.

Michael C.M. Wilson is head of the Asia Pacific Fixed Income Research Group at J.P. Morgan & Company. Prior to joining this group, he established J.P. Morgan's sales and trading research function in London and served as deputy head of the U.S. Fixed Income Research Group in New York. Before joining J.P. Morgan, he worked at Orion Royal Bank, where he was responsible for trading research. Mr. Wilson holds a B.A. in operational research and statistics from St. John's College in Cambridge.

Robert G. Zielinski, CFA, is head of global sectoral research and Asian bank research at Jardine Fleming Securities, Limited, Singapore. Previously, he headed research for Jardine Fleming, Thailand, and served as an analyst of Japanese bank securities for Jardine Fleming, Japan. Mr. Zielinski was voted the number one and number two bank analyst in Asia by *Institutional Investor* in 1996 and 1997, respectively. He holds B.S. and M.S. degrees from the Massachusetts Institute of Technology and an M.B.A. from Harvard Business School.

Asian Equity Investing: An Overview

When selecting attractive stocks and achieving higher incremental returns in domestic stock markets becomes increasingly difficult, investors tend to shed their home-country biases and allocate a higher percentage of their assets to global financial markets in search of more attractive returns. Given that Asian economies have experienced, and may continue to experience, higher economic growth rates than most developed countries, Asian financial markets offer opportunities for attractive equity market returns for investors willing to take additional risk and willing to spend additional time researching companies and studying the structure of these markets.

As investors allocate additional assets to global markets, and Asian markets in particular, portfolio managers can apply a variety of approaches for investing—from top-down and bottom-up methodologies to style investing. Regardless of the investment approach used, successful investing in Asian markets requires an understanding of how each market fits within the global framework and how this framework influences country and security selection. Effective research techniques and relevant valuation methods help investors evaluate potential investments and separate attractive from potential problem investments—that is, the winners from the losers. Before implementing style investing, investors and portfolio managers should assess the benefits of various investment management approaches and styles as applied in Asian markets. An important aspect of this assessment involves deciding whether style investing is an effective investment approach in non-U.S. equity markets. Finally, investors and portfolio managers must deal with ubiquitous currency volatility in Asian markets in order to protect portfolio returns and control portfolio risk.

Asian Markets: The Big Picture

A crucial step in a successful investment strategy for an Asian equity portfolio is an evaluation of Asian markets in the context of the global economy. Having a strong understanding of how Asian economies are interrelated with the world economy gives the portfolio manager an edge and an opportunity to add value through country and industry selection. David Roche examines the October 1997 Asian currency crisis, identifies the roots of the problems in East Asia, provides a straightforward recipe for recovery, and assesses the impact of the Asian crisis on the global economy.

Roche points out that the Asian crisis will have a significant deflationary effect on real global economies, especially Japan's, and will divert capital from East Asia and Latin America into the safe haven of the United States. Roche explains that the Asian crisis is really two crises: an external deficit crisis, which is the result of limited export growth and a high propensity to import, and a capital overhang crisis, which is the result of low interest rates, surplus capital, and marginally unproductive investments. The cure to the crisis in East Asia is straightforward and involves floating currencies, tighter fiscal policies, a liberalized financial sector, and increased competition through deregulation. Although the East Asian crisis will not drive the global economy into a recession, it will slow Asian economic growth. The overall impact on the global economy will be higher risk premiums, higher interest rates, lower economic growth, and lower profit growth. After a painful period of adjustment, Roche believes that Asian economies could experience double-digit growth rates.

Research Techniques and Fundamental Analysis

The amount of analytical research needed to evaluate Asian equities depends on how developed the market is. Robert Zielinski points out that the level of research needed in an emerging market initially involves a market presence and company visits; later, as the market matures and commissions decline, the research function also includes company and industry analysis followed by thematic research reports. Zielinski highlights the major challenges associated with researching and valuing Asian companies and describes three phases of research.

Major data problems, which include selecting an appropriate discount rate, unreliable corporate disclosures, and limited data, affect the analyst's ability to research Asian companies. In spite of data problems, microanalysis, macroanalysis, and quantitative analysis can add value. Zielinski does not underestimate the value of visiting a company or a development site. Company visits easily and quickly confirm or dispel concerns that valuation models may not detect, such as mountains of unsold inventory or unoccupied real estate developments. After all, the Petronas Twin Towers in Malaysia are currently not only the tallest buildings in the world but also the tallest vacant buildings in the world.

In terms of industry analysis, Zielinski explains that understanding the paradigm in which the industry operates is crucial in Asian markets because capital structures, operating strategies, and entrepreneurships (especially in the real estate industry) are quite different from those of U.S. corporations. Macroanalysis and quantitative studies provide analysts with additional tools to identify opportunities and problems or make comparisons at the industry and country levels. Finally, Zielinski shows how new valuation techniques can complement traditional valuation models by dealing with industry-specific issues.

Style Investing

Style investing has been widely accepted by managers, clients, and consultants in the United States, but whether styles can be identified and exploited in markets outside the United States has long been debated. In a joint presentation, Richard Bernstein and Nigel Tupper provide a clear definition of style investing and illustrate how style investing works in U.S. and Asian equity markets.

Traditional style categories in the United States encompass growth, value, size, and yield factors; styles tend to rotate in and out of favor within a given market. In the first part of the presentation, Bernstein states that style investing is more than simply value and growth investing; style is a market segment with common characteristics that perform similarly over market cycles. He discusses how structural, psychological, and informational asymmetry within markets can explain the relative performance of stocks. Most importantly, Bernstein illustrates how styles rotate in cycles within the United States and explains how profits, credit, and interest rates affect style rotation. Finally, he points out the significance of the earnings expectation life cycle and demonstrates what separates good managers from bad managers in terms of this cycle.

In the second part of the presentation, Tupper applies this analysis of style investing to Australia, Hong Kong, Malaysia, and Singapore and illustrates how style rotation and profit cycles work in these markets. He first looks at each market in terms of style rotation and then looks at the profit cycle, value strategies, growth strategies, the predictability of brokers' optimism, and a strategy based on earnings momentum, value, and optimism. Tupper observes that value and growth strategies work in Asia, although the success of these strategies varies with each market.

Robert Schwob looks at style analysis in various non-U.S. markets and finds that style analysis is a relevant and practical portfolio management tool that must be carefully applied with regard to local market characteristics. Because assessing the degree to which styles work in different countries is important, Schwob describes a verification procedure for judging the relevance of each style. This procedure includes using a Monte Carlo technique to determine the probability that returns can be explained by a specific style factor and not by random portfolio construction. Schwob discusses the importance of neutralizing the effects of sector imbalances on style analysis and points out that sector adjustment removes the effects of pronounced industrial cycles, interest rate movements, or exchange rate movements on specific market sectors. Schwob, much like Tupper, concludes that key style factors are relevant in non-U.S. markets, even after sector adjustment, and suggests that a bottom-up style analysis provides important details about a manager's style orientation and insight into a manager's investment philosophy.

Alternative Equity Strategies

Many different approaches, such as style investing, can be used for successful equity investing in Asia. Donald Krueger provides a different perspective on Asian equity investing and presents the investment decision-making process for a hedge fund that invests in Asia ex-Japan. Krueger welcomes the volatility in Asian ex-Japan markets because it creates opportunities for patient investors to provide liquidity—for a premium, of course—in the marketplace.

According to Krueger, a successful investment has several components. The ability to analyze a company's fundamentals, an attractive valuation, and a catalyst that will result in an upward revaluation are necessary conditions for a stock to be included in his portfolio. Adequate liquidity and sufficient diversification among stocks and countries are also necessary criteria for the portfolio to meet redemptions and control risk. The final component involves the careful application of strategic hedges to protect portfolio returns. Krueger adds that patience is a virtue in Asian markets and cautions that a disciplined approach to investing needs time to work.

Currency Risk Management

Currency risk management is one of the most important tasks of global portfolio managers because of its significant effect on risk and return in the short run. Michael Wilson discusses currency management for Asian equity portfolios in light of the October 1997 Asian currency crises.

Wilson cautions Asian equity investors that volatility is here to stay and predicts that systematic hedging of all Asian currency exposures is suboptimal and will not reduce volatility because of the very low correlations between Asian currencies and equity markets. He suggests that selective hedging in Asian markets may be the best approach for managing currency risk, but he warns investors to select the most liquid hedging vehicle and to consider the cost of hedging. Several approaches, including break-even standard deviations, quantifying pressure on foreign exchange rates, and analyzing foreign exchange regime shifts, can help investors decide when to hedge currency risk. Nevertheless, investors must first think about the impact of short-term currency volatility, interest rate differentials, and currency trends on the hedging decision.

Conclusion

In spite of short-term volatility, Asian equity markets will continue to offer potentially attractive investment opportunities to patient and disciplined global investors. The key to successful investing in these markets is to view them in a global context, develop an appropriate investment strategy or style, adapt research and valuation techniques to each market and industry paradigm, and manage currency risk. Just as portfolio managers evaluate investments using the total portfolio approach—evaluating each investment's contribution to overall portfolio risk and return—investors should assess Asian markets in the context of the global economy. In this proceedings, the authors bring together an important blend of experience, skill, and insight to help readers evaluate the opportunities and risks in Asian equity markets (in terms of the unique characteristics and structure of each market), develop their own investment strategy or style, and discover new ways to add value to the investment process.

Asian Markets in a Global Framework

David S. Roche, CFA
Chair
Independent Strategy, Ltd.

Throughout the turmoil in Asian financial markets in 1997, the U.S. dollar has remained a safe haven, drawing capital from Latin America and East Asia. The root of the problems in East Asia lies in exceptionally high external deficits and low capital productivity; however, the recipe for recovery is straightforward. The overall impact of the East Asian crisis will be higher risk premiums, higher interest rates, lower economic growth, and lower growth in profits. But the long-term future looks bright; Asian countries could experience double-digit growth rates after a period of painful adjustment.

No one entirely understands the interaction between the recent Asian crisis and the global crisis. Normally, one would expect a global crisis to bring about a crisis in a particular country. In this case, an Asian crisis has brought about a crisis in Hong Kong, which has brought about a global crisis. Although I do not have all the answers, I can at least point out some of the factors that have brought about this chain reaction of crises.

In this presentation, I will discuss the global market setting—what is going on in the financial markets today, and why, at Independent Strategy, we think it is different from 1987. Then, I will examine the Asian crisis, notably the external debt problems and capital problems, and address some of the cures. Finally, I will show how the Asian crisis connects into the global crisis.

Asian Markets Today

Because of the turmoil in Asian financial markets in the fall of 1997, observers are naturally tempted to make connections between the events of 1987 and the events of 1997, but at Independent Strategy, we see more dissimilarities than similarities.

Securities Markets. The security markets of 1997 are very different from the markets of 1987, and the correct strategies for investors are different as well. Investors have been trained to rush out and buy equities on dips, which was the right thing to do in 1987, although that was a rather big dip. That strategy is probably the wrong one to use in 1997, partly because we think the global markets will continue to fall. Instead, we think the market is bullish for bonds worldwide.

Central banks are not going to react the same way in 1997 as they did in 1987. Interest rates cannot be reduced. In Japan, for example, interest rates can hardly go any lower than they already have, and in Europe, where the economies are finally recovering, the idea is to increase interest rates ahead of European Monetary Union (EMU). By having the Bundesbank hike rates, the gap on short-term interest rates in Europe will narrow. Thus, we believe that the crash of 1997, unlike the crash of 1987, will have a significant deflationary effect on the real global economy.

If central bankers are not going to cut interest rates and inject massive liquidity into the system, as they did in 1987, then the response to what is happening now in economic terms will be more drawn out than it was in 1987. The return of liquidity to chase up asset prices is not going to happen soon, and the economic effects of wealth destruction in financial markets is going to be felt at the level of real demand in economies—particularly in the U.S. economy—more severely than in 1987. Therefore, we think that equity markets face further corrections, simply because profits are going to get hit and interest rates are not going to fall at the short end in the same way they did in 1987.

We are bullish on bonds because we think that the next surprise coming out of the market downturns is going to be that the markets have done what the central bankers talked about doing for them: They will have taken the cream off the top of this economic cycle, and as a result, we will see few, if any, increases in long-term interest rates around the world.

Currency Markets. In our view, the safe-haven status of the U.S. dollar will remain. Capital will continue to flow out of Latin America and East Asia toward the United States. We plan on remaining short most emerging market currencies. Ultimately, we think that the Hong Kong dollar will lose its peg to the U.S dollar when China allows the renminbi to fall, which it will have to do within the next couple of years. If the renminbi falls, the Hong Kong dollar peg will make no sense. The idea of having two national currencies, one that is strong and represents 6 million people and one that is weak and represents 1.2 billion people (with the weaker one paying for the luxury items of the stronger one), would be politically unacceptable and economic nonsense. So, over time, we have no doubt that the Hong Kong dollar will be unpegged, but at least for the next year, the Hong Kong authorities will pay practically any price, in terms of interest rates, to maintain the peg, which creates a negative real estate market in Hong Kong.

If the Asian crisis is to have one real macroeconomic impact in a deflationary sense, it will be with Japan. The situation in Asia, and in the financial markets in general, will undermine the fragile confidence of the already withering Japanese economy and prolong what may have been a short downturn after tax increases into a real recession. If Japan is forced into a recession, it has absolutely no option but to pursue a policy based on further fiscal stimulus and, of course, further devaluation of the yen.

Market Liquidity. In general, we believe that liquidity is tightening globally, partly through wealth destruction and partly because broad money has recently been lagging economic growth in Organization for Economic Cooperation and Development (OECD) countries. This tightening of liquidity negatively affects our opinion of emerging markets (which are having difficulty procuring funds to finance their growth and boost their asset prices) and industrial commodities, particularly copper, because the biggest growth disappointments are likely to be in the emergent, industrializing economies, which are likely to cut their consumption of industrial commodities relatively dramatically.

East Asian Crises

East Asia really has two crises. One is the crisis of excessive external deficits, and the other is a domestic capital crisis.

External Deficit Crisis. Low export growth coupled with an extremely high propensity to import and fast domestic demand growth have created exceptionally high external deficits in East Asia. The task of reducing these deficits is immense.

Going forward, GDP growth will be limited to export growth divided by import elasticity, which has been extraordinarily high in East Asia. To reduce deficits, exports have to grow as fast, or faster, than imports, which have traditionally grown 1.5 times as fast as domestic demand growth. East Asian economies, particularly Hong Kong and the Philippines, have high import elasticities to real GDP growth. Based on the present elasticities of imports, exports would have to grow by 9 percent a year, in volume terms, for the GDP to be able to expand by 6 percent a year without expanding the current account deficits as a proportion of GDP. That task is an immense challenge for these economies, which are hardly achieving any export growth, as **Figure 1** shows.

The external financing needs, or net financing requirements (NFRs), are the sum of the current account deficit, debt servicing, and net inward foreign direct investment. In East Asia, excluding the People's Republic of China (PRC) and Singapore, NFRs doubled from a deficit of –2 percent of GDP in 1993 to –4 percent of GDP in 1995 and 1996, as shown in **Figure 2**. In our judgment, NFRs will improve but slowly. Because the NFR is the major determinant of the premium that East Asia has to pay, in terms of interest rates to attract foreign capital, we think that its slow improvement will mean that East Asian interest rates will remain much higher than in the past.

The trade deficits, which are the kernel of the external financing issue in Asia, are not cyclical but structural problems. The older East Asian Tigers' share of the OECD market is either declining or stagnating. All of the gains made in percentage share of OECD imports by East Asian countries in recent years were made by the PRC and to a lesser extent the Philippines. Many people believe the root of the problem is that the PRC competes with East Asian exports not only at the low end of the scale (e.g., textiles) but also at the high end of the scale (e.g., information technology products).

Although the internationalization of PRC exports has had a big effect on East Asian exports, the effect of exports from the newly emergent economies in Latin America and Eastern Europe has been much greater. As shown in **Figure 3**, over the 1989–96 period, Latin America and Eastern Europe gained import share of U.S. and western European imports, respectively, at the expense of East Asia, which was a fairly dramatic shift, further underscoring the immensity of the challenge to increase growth.

Capital Overhang Crisis. East Asia's second

Figure 1. East Asia: Growth in Value of International Trade, 1990–96

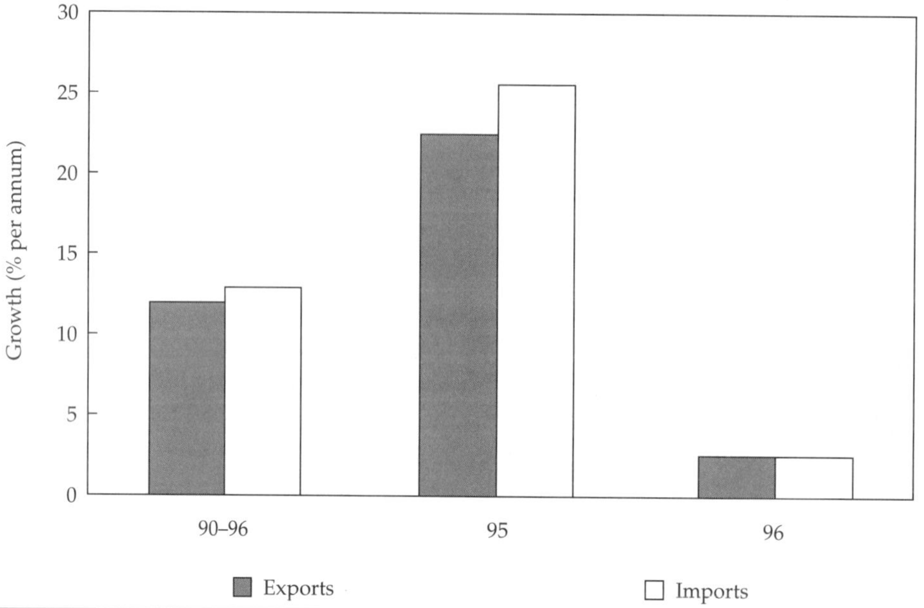

Growth (% per annum)
30
25
20
15
10
5
0
90–96
95
96
Exports
Imports

Note: Data cover Hong Kong, South Korea, Malaysia, Singapore, China, Taiwan, and Thailand.
Source: Based on data from the *WTO World Trade Report*.

Figure 2. East Asia's Net External Financing Requirements as Percentage of GDP, 1990–99

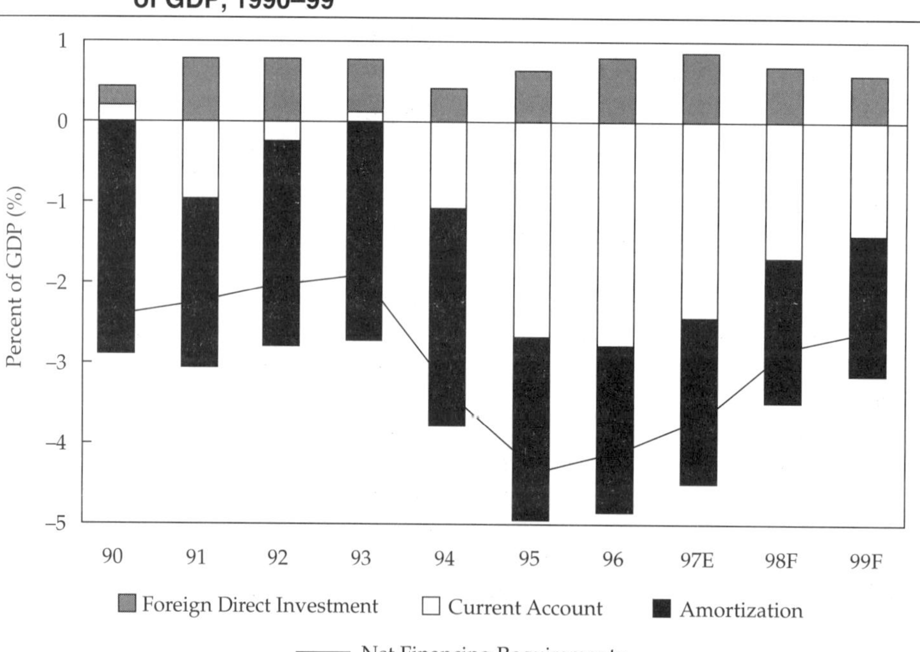

Note: Data exclude China and Singapore; 1997 data are estimated, and 1999 data are forecasted.
Sources: Based on data from the IMF and World Bank.

major problem is capital overhang. The dollar block's almost-fixed-peg currency arrangements were important to East Asia's development. Having an exchange rate virtually fixed to a major world currency lent enormous credibility to young countries' monetary policies. These countries attracted foreign capital because foreign investors experienced little exchange rate risk from investing in these countries; domestically, rich people kept their capital at home because they found little advantage from investing

Figure 3. Index of Emerging Markets' Share of U.S. and European Union Total Imports, 1989–96

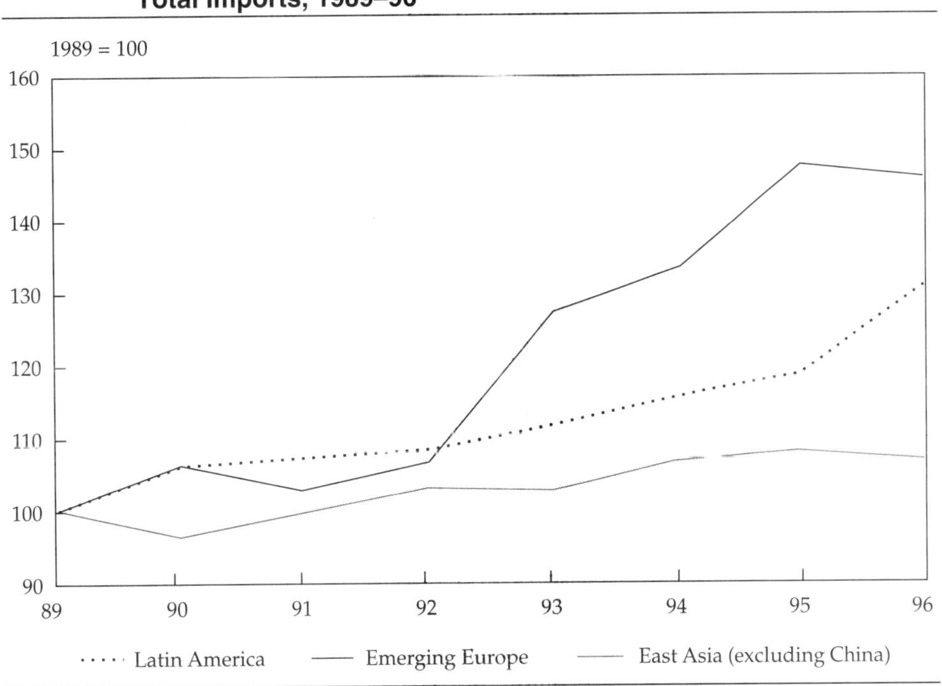

abroad. But as East Asian countries developed, these advantages were outweighed by the disadvantages of such an exchange rate regime. In particular, at the peak of the U.S. economic cycle, when East Asia's exports were booming and the United States was running a big current account deficit, the world was being flooded with dollars and East Asia got swamped with liquidity. Consequently, the East Asian central banks had to keep their interest rates low to prevent their currencies from rising under the pressure of the inflow of U.S. dollars and other foreign capital. Low interest rates made capital plentiful and cheap, which led to overheating and investments in marginal and unproductive projects.

This problem was compounded by a fatal mistake made by the East Asian central banks in the four countries now in the most difficulty—Indonesia, Malaysia, South Korea, and Thailand. They tried to fix their exchange rates and target domestic monetary supply growth and interest rates all at the same time. Central banks can hit only one target at a time, so by trying to hit multiple targets, they were often trapped and tempted into using sterilized intervention, which actually worsened the distortions of excessive capital inflows into these countries.

The key problems of capital overhang are evident in Asia today. Excessive capital inflows encourage unsustainable NFRs (shown in **Figure 4**), burgeoning exposure to short-term foreign bank debt (shown in **Figure 5**), and excessive borrowing from foreign banks and overseas capital markets by the private sector (shown in **Figure 6**). This debt has now become expensive foreign money and often unserviceable foreign liabilities. The corporate sector did not accumulate foreign debt directly; rather, they converted foreign capital inflows into cheap local currency credit and created domestic liquidity and asset bubbles, as in Malaysia. Bank credit was also allocated to nonproductive assets, such as real estate and the stock market, particularly in Hong Kong, which makes the real economy and the stock market much more vulnerable to high interest rates.

With interest rates and the cost of capital arbitrarily low, borrowers and investors of capital in those countries, convinced by the propaganda of their own politicians and central banks, thought that no exchange rate risk was associated with those borrowings. Therefore, they did what any entrepreneur would do: continued to invest until the marginal return on capital equaled the marginal cost, because that is how the investor gets richest, which is exactly what happened. Recently, the marginal cost of that capital has jumped, and a rather large amount of the assets that were invested are underwater. Cheap capital became wasted capital and resulted in returns on investments that were less than the cost of the debt capital itself, let alone the required return on equity capital. In five of the seven major East Asian countries shown in **Figure 7**, the return on capital in 1997 is well below what is required to service even short-term debt, and for some countries it has been for years.

Figure 4. Forecasted NFRs as a Percentage of GDP, 1997

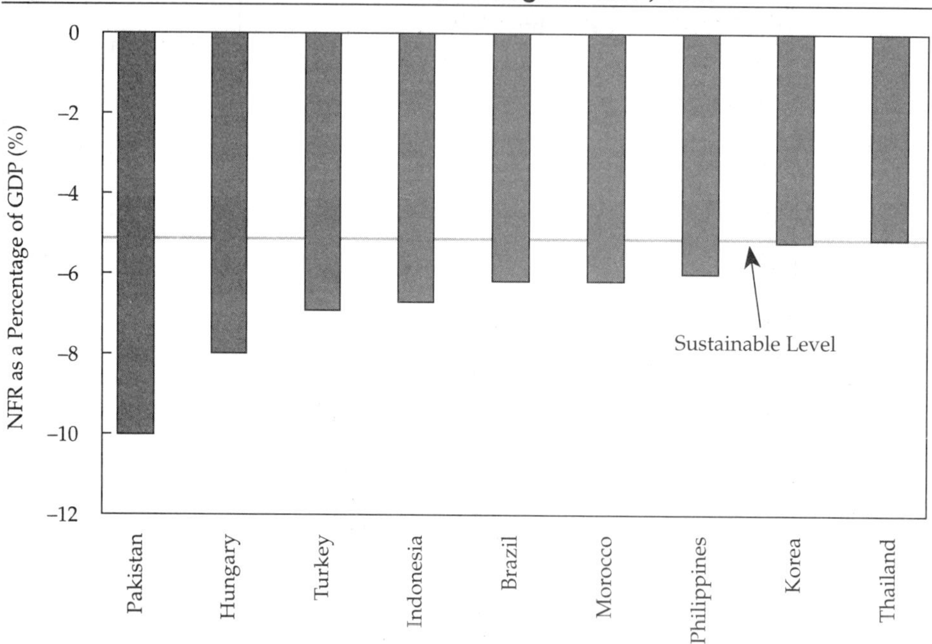

Figure 5. East Asian Borrowing from Foreign Banks, December 1995–June 1997

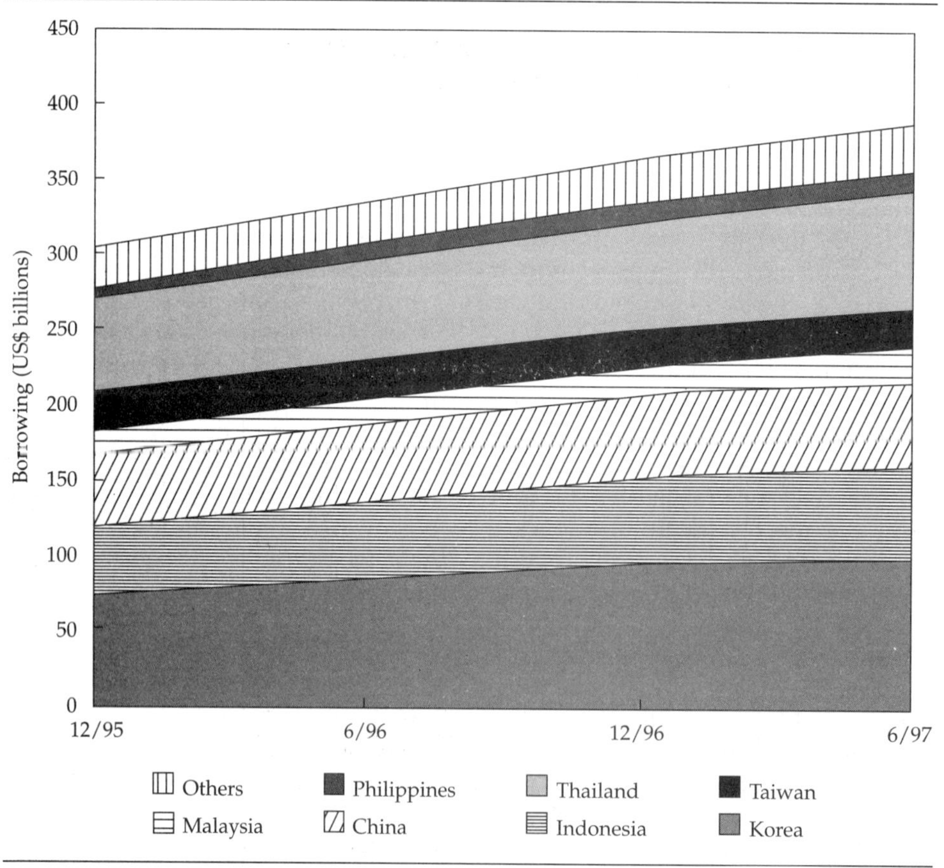

Figure 6. Borrowing from Foreign Banks and Other Foreign Debt as a Percentage of Exports, 1996

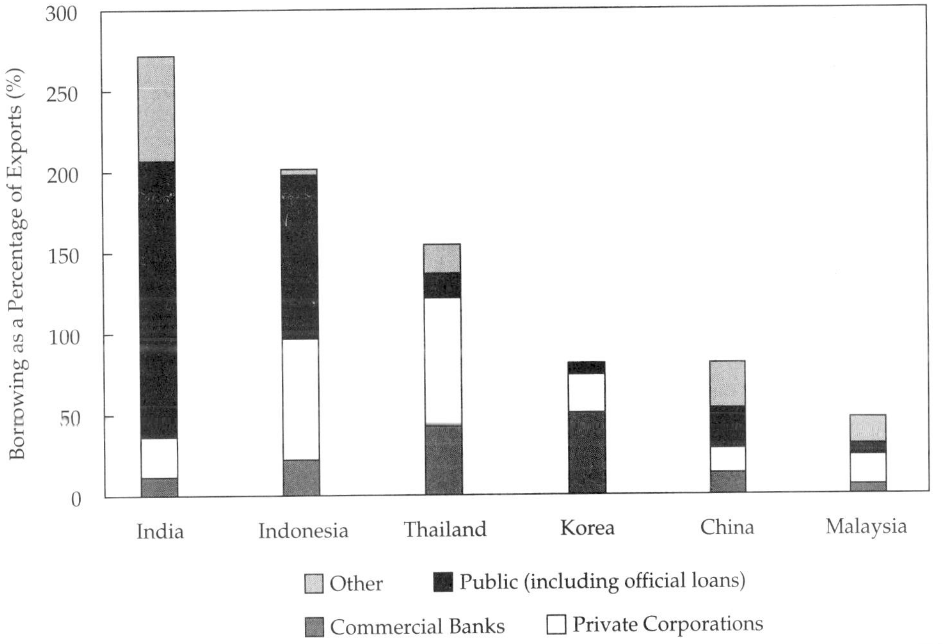

Sources: The Bank for International Settlements and the IMF.

Figure 7. Return on Equity as a Percentage of Three-Month Interest Rates, December 1995–December 1997

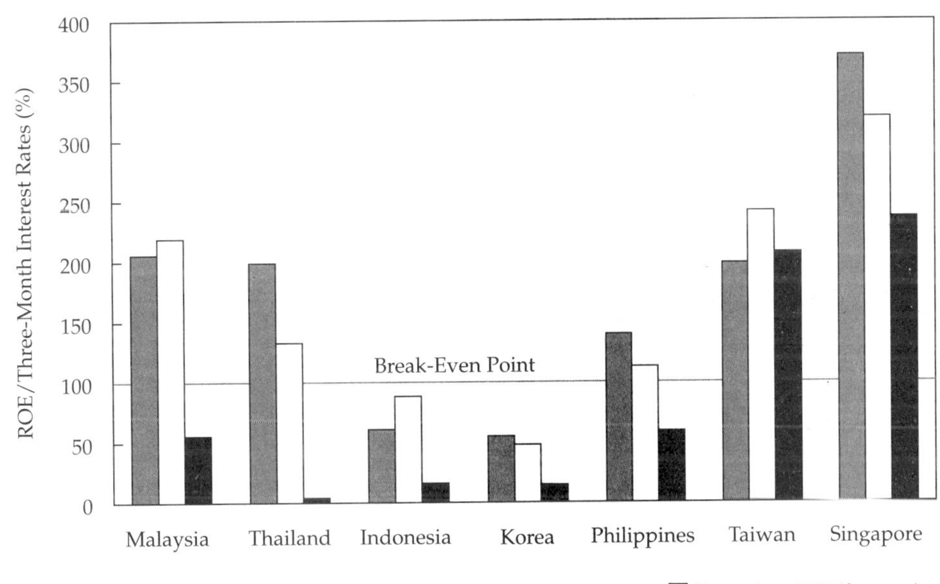

Note: The break-even point is where ROE equals three-month interest rates.

Declining capital productivity is a big problem and essentially means that more and more capital is needed to produce less and less growth. Some countries in the region, such as Indonesia and Hong Kong, have actually been improving since 1991, but in countries such as Thailand, Malaysia, and Korea the ratio of the amount of capital needed to produce each extra unit of output has been dramatically and steadily worsening, as shown in **Figure 8**.

East Asia: The Cures

Currency crises always have, with varying proportions, two ingredients: an excessive external deficit and a stock of unproductive assets financed in the wrong way. The recipe for recovery is straightforward:

- *Float currencies.*
- *Keep interest rates fairly high but lower than needed to defend the currency itself.* The reason for keeping interest rates high is to ration capital and ensure that what is invested, is invested productively. Furthermore, high interest rates prevent the effects of devaluation from working their way into domestic inflation through an overly lax monetary policy. At the same time, fiscal policies need to be tight, and the country needs to run a surplus to increase the national savings rate and thus reduce the current account deficit, which is equal to domestic savings less investment.
- *Tighten fiscal policies to run a surplus and improve the current account.*
- *Reform, regulate, and liberalize the financial sector.* Undoubtedly, one of the reasons why East Asia became so dependent on foreign capital was the poor structure of the financial sector, which was ineffective at matching huge stocks of domestic savings with productive opportunities. The result was an overdependence on foreign capital. In reality, domestic sources should be able to finance a much greater degree of Asian development and growth.
- *Deregulate the economy to raise competitiveness.* A country with a currency crisis needs to deregulate its economy and raise competitiveness. The one way to foster competitive exports is to allow imports to compete. Only by fully plugging a country's economy into the world economic system and allowing domestic prices to be influenced by international prices are the signals given in the domestic market that the comparative advantages and the real skills of the economy will be properly allocated. At that point, a country will end up not only with a competitive domestic market but also, of course, with a competitive export sector.
- *Increase domestic content of infrastructure projects and exports.* If one single step could be taken in Asia to improve the productivity of capital, it would be to open up every single infrastructure contract to public bidding on a properly audited basis. Undoubtedly, the greatest waste of capital is in the way vast infrastructure projects are decided without a competitive, open, and transparent bidding process, although notable exceptions do exist. The chances of seeing that transformation happen are probably slim, but that change is needed.

Figure 8. Change in Asian Productivity of Capital, 1991–96

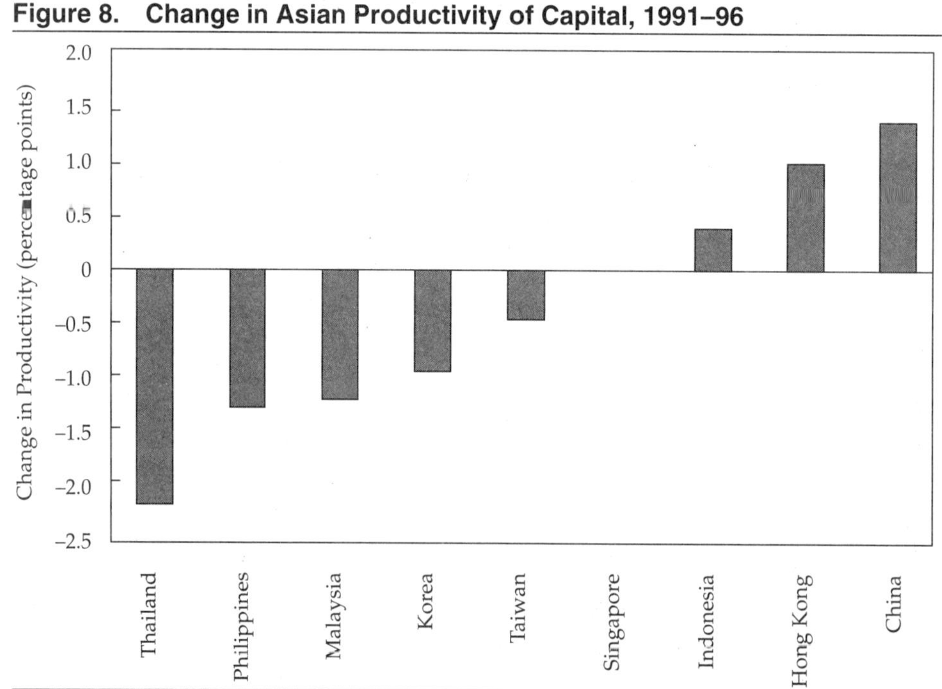

Note: Productivity of capital equals the investment-to-GDP ratio divided by GDP growth (five-year moving average).

- *Raise and improve domestic research and development spending.*

Although the cures for currency crises are straightforward, avoiding further mistakes will be tricky.

Impact of the Asian Crisis

One can find both good and bad news when looking at the East Asian crisis in relation to the global economy. The good news is that East Asia is not about to drive the global economy into recession by affecting trade flows and by creating bad debts in the OECD countries' banking systems. Rather, East Asia's deflationary effect on the OECD countries will come from Asia's effect on global financial markets being passed on to the real economies of the OECD countries.

Exports. The impact of the East Asian crises on OECD countries is likely to be slight. The whole East Asian region represents about 8.5 percent of global GDP and about 18 percent of world trade, and the problem countries (i.e., Korea, Thailand, Malaysia, the Philippines, and Indonesia) represent only about 4 percent of world GDP and about 6.5 percent of world trade. Exports to the problem countries represent substantially less than 1 percent of all the major OECD economies' GDP, as shown in **Table 1**. Even in the case of Japan, exports to problem Asian countries are a low percentage of its GDP, and because Asian exports to the problem countries are a low percentage of the exports themselves, from a trade point of view, the overall economic impact on OECD economies is likely to be quite small.

The impact of the East Asian crises on Asia itself, however, is obviously more severe. A 30 percent fall in exports to the problem countries would have a huge impact on Asian growth, as shown in **Figure 9**. The almost 12 percent drop in real GDP for Singapore

Table 1. Share of Total Exports by Region and as a Percentage of Exporters' GDP, 1996

Region	Exports to East Asia[a]	Exports to Problem Asia	Problem Asia/ Exporters' GDP
Europe	4.5%	0.9%	0.6%
United States	18.1	9.4	0.7
Japan	42.1	19.1	1.7

[a]Includes China.

Note: Problem Asia includes Indonesia, Malaysia, South Korea, Thailand, and the Philippines.

Figure 9. The Effect on Real GDP Growth from a Fall in the Demand for Exports from East Asian Problem Countries

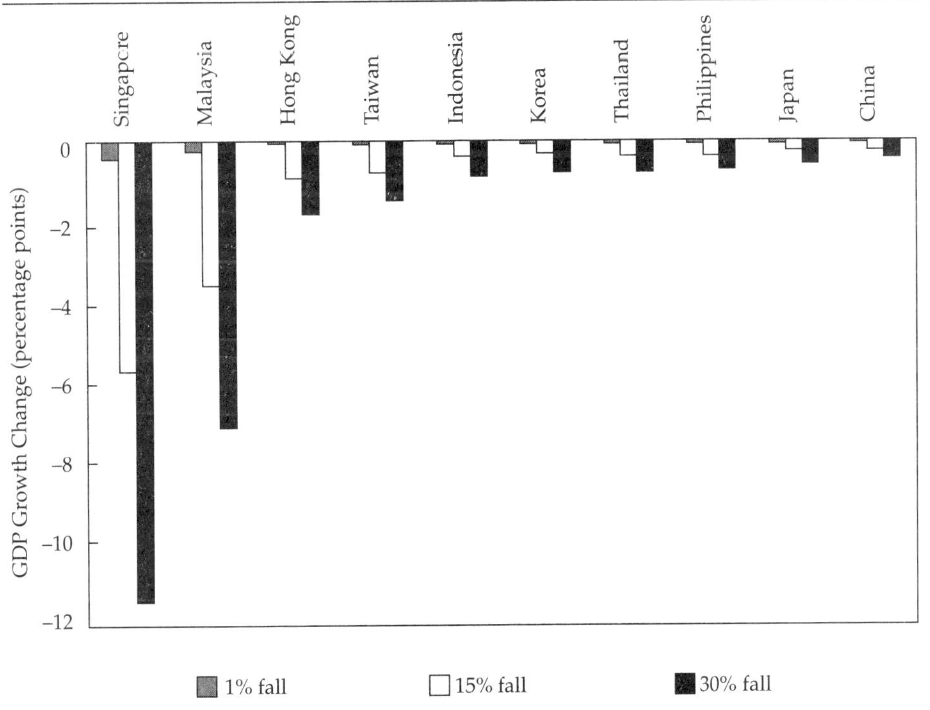

in this scenario is overly alarmist, of course, because a substantial portion (perhaps as much as two-thirds) of exports from Singapore to the problem countries do not end up being consumed in those countries. These exports actually get used in other products, which are then exported to the United States or Europe. So, effectively, a trade circuit exists. The devaluations occurring in the problem countries of East Asia make these manufacturing operations, which are basically Singapore offshore operations for subsequent product export to OECD countries, more competitive as long as wage inflation can be contained. The amount of exports that will actually suffer from a big slowdown in the East Asian economies is small, as a proportion of total exports, but will nevertheless mean that growth in Singapore is probably going to fall by 1 or 2 percentage points.

Banking Flows. If anybody were to go broke because of the problems in East Asia, it would be Japanese banks, but this event is unlikely. The problem countries of East Asia represent less than 4 percent of global international bank lending (i.e., every country's bank lending outside its own domestic market). The problem countries of East Asia represent about 6 percent of Japanese banks' international lending. If 30 percent of all loans to Thailand by Japanese banks and 15 percent of Japanese banks' loans to other East Asian countries failed, the Japanese banks would lose 1 percent of their loan book. Because much of Japanese banks' lending to the East Asian countries is effectively Japanese banks lending to Japanese corporations producing for export in those countries, this hypothesis is extreme and, I think, probably not a cataclysmic one. Keep in mind that so far, Japanese banks have admitted to losing 8 percent of all their loans in the Tokyo property market (the real figure is probably 15 percent), and they are still more or less going strong. So, it is unlikely that the additional losses in Asia would cause a mammoth banking collapse in the country most exposed to the region outside the region itself, Japan. What any additional losses are likely to do is encourage the Bank of Japan to continue with an extremely lax monetary policy for a little longer. Therefore, East Asia will not bring down the global banking system. East Asia will simply bring down a few of its own banking systems.

Global Capital Markets. At Independent Strategy, we believe that the impact of the East Asian capital market crises will be higher risk premiums, higher interest rates, lower economic growth, and lower profit growth. The markets are also coming to that conclusion. We do not think that the global economy will climb to the peak of this cycle and overheat. The most likely immediate outcome for the global economy is that short-term interest rates will not go up by as much as we previously thought, if at all, because demand will be capped by the wealth effects in some of the major markets, particularly in the United States, and by the increased fragility of the Japanese economy as fears of recession start to increase. The lower interest rate scenario gives at least some help to Asia but not a lot; even without a big increase in U.S. interest rates, the risk premium on capital flowing into Asia has actually risen.

Therefore, despite the fact that we expect interest rates to rise on a global scale, we do not think that this change in rates will be a major sign of relief for the Asian markets, particularly because the U.S. dollar will remain a strong safe-haven currency, which makes for greater pressure on the interest rates of those countries with weaker financial systems and weaker currencies. Furthermore, weaker growth around the world will hit profit growth. Already, according to our statistics, in most of the OECD economies—Europe, certainly, and the United States—the share of profit in national income has ceased to rise. Of course, the share of profit in national income could not rise forever. It has been increasing for 10 years, which is quite a long time. But if it continued to increase forever, it would absorb the whole of national income; nothing would be left for the masses, and capitalism would collapse, which is what Karl Marx predicted. Effectively, the topping out of share of profit in national income, which is also reflected, in our view, in the rates of increase in corporate profitability around the world, contributes to growth and to margin improvement. In the corporate sector, we saw that margin improvement was slowing down and thus most of the growth in corporate profits was being driven by volume increases, gains in output, and world growth. If world growth slows down, then we do not expect that the productivity miracle, which drove these corporate profits higher as a share of national income and improved the margins, will be able to compensate for lower volume growth. Therefore, in most equity markets outside East Asia, we think that in the next couple of years the average rate of growth in earnings, profits, EPS, etc. will be decidedly single-digit, which means, of course, that this scenario of slowing world growth and sticky interest rates is effectively not a bull-market scenario for equities.

Asian Capital Markets: The Future

The markets of Asia will still go through a period of painful adjustment, but I am absolutely convinced that after that adjustment, the growth rates in these countries will remain much higher than those of the OECD countries and that Asian living standards will catch up with those in OECD countries. The rates for

P/E per unit of long-term sustainable growth are now quite reasonable for Asia compared with many other world markets, as shown in **Figure 10**. Sustainable earnings growth rates, looking beyond the next couple of years of painful adjustment in this region, are still probably double-digit figures.

These changes can happen, but nothing is automatic. In this region, we have already seen countries constrained by foreign debt and good sense, such as Indonesia and the Philippines, mapping out hard-option policy responses to the current crisis. The hard-option policy responses are those of supply-side reform: cutting fiscal expenditures, tight monetary policies, and defending the exchange rate with high interest rates. Those are the changes that will get countries out of trouble much sooner and back to growth in a better state than countries such as Malaysia and Korea, which have domestic credit-driven asset bubbles that encourage them to choose soft-option economic policies that will not work.

The single biggest danger to this scenario is actually political. To be successful, a currency devaluation has to achieve two objectives. First, it must reduce living standards and transfer national income from wage earners to profits. That change is the way to make capital more profitable—enable companies to have the cash flow they need to work off the capital overhang of unwise investment in the past—and it is the way to make exports more competitive again. The second objective, which must be fulfilled, is to stop devaluation from becoming inflation, particularly wage inflation. If inflation happens, the nominal exchange rate may have been devalued but the real exchange rate will actually end up exactly where it started, or worse. Domestic inflation in a country will rise above that of its trading partners, and the country will have simply distorted the pricing system to the detriment of capital investment. The economy will enter into a period of long-run slow growth, such as I think could happen in the soft-option countries in this region (e.g., Malaysia and Korea).

Devaluations, which cut living standards and transfer national income from wage earners to profits, are not an automatic result of the deliberations going on at the highest levels in this region today. A devaluation poses an enormous challenge for an administration that has to communicate a very hard message to people, whose expectations of constantly rising living standards will be disappointed. All of East Asia's political institutions and bureaucracies are unlikely to have clear knowledge of the message they have to impart or how to impart it. If they do not express the message well and show leadership, then I believe that a very sharp difference will be drawn between the countries that manage to achieve the hard option of currency devaluations and the countries that choose to follow soft options. In certain cases, the political systems will actually not withstand the amount of tension that will be created by failure.

Figure 10. P/E per Unit of Long-Term Sustainable EPS Growth: Various Countries, 1997

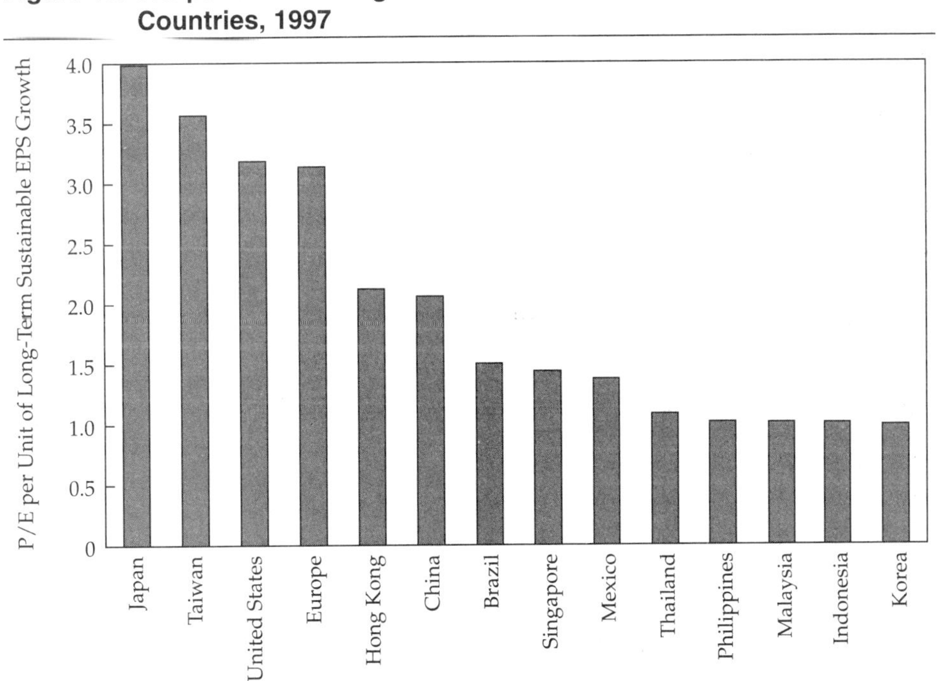

Question and Answer Session

David Roche

Question: Why are open capital account economies, such as Thailand, the Philippines, and Indonesia, prone to excessive capital spending and crises and countries with closed capital accounts, such as Taiwan and India, not?

Roche: You are perfectly right to point out the difference between an India or a Taiwan with a closed capital account and a country such as Thailand or Malaysia with an open capital account. But the country with the worst financial crisis and the biggest banking crisis also has a closed capital account—Korea. So, the issue is not about being closed or open. The issue is how a country runs its financial system.

In many cases, countries made errors in reforming and liberalizing their financial systems, by which I mean removing all barriers as to how investors borrow and invest in countries, but the regulation of the risks associated with making such a great step were not put in place. For example, if you went to Thailand two years ago, you would have been told that offshore loans from the Bangkok International Bank Facility were entirely safe. You would have been told that, although they were all rated short-term capital, they really were long-term capital and were all given to nice Japanese producers by Japanese banks borrowing in U.S. dollars.

Today, we know that what happened in Thailand was that people borrowed at very low U.S. rates, very low compared with the domestic rates. The problem in Thailand is not the liberalization; it is the regulation of the liberalization. Thailand had absolutely no rules about who had to hedge what or how the risk exposure was to be handled. So, open markets do not endanger the stability of countries by themselves. The real issue is making the financial system properly regulated so that it is transparent, the risks are controlled, etc.

Question: To what extent do you think global investors were responsible for creating the boom in East Asia?

Roche: Certainly, global investors were, to a degree, responsible for what happened in East Asia. There is no point in pretending otherwise. Most people who visited East Asia and who were investing money in this region had knowledge that was limited to a superficial week-long visit. Not only did the investors act unwisely, but the economic policies of the countries receiving this investment were also unwise.

When the going was good, these countries should have broken the link with the U.S. dollar, allowed their currencies to appreciate, forced their producers to move out of knitting into making computers (thus getting rid of the low value-added production to which they were no longer suited on a competitive basis), and allowed monetary policy to match what they needed. In other words, they actually needed to have a much more stringent monetary policy and needed to make it more risky for people to flood the country with money, because the currency could go up as well as down. They needed to allow the pricing of money to give a clear signal to their economies. De-linking now has resulted in all the dangers of badly handled devaluations and falling living standards.

Perhaps the most unwise decision on the part of these countries was to maintain the dollar-block relationships that had outlived their economic usefulness. And perhaps the most unwise decision on the part of investors was to assume that they could put their money in and have it always come out at the same exchange rate.

Question: Do the current crises legitimize the imposition of capital controls in the short term?

Roche: I do not think so. Take two examples. First, why did economic liberalization—letting market pricing systems work in their own way, freely—take so long to implement in Japan? Japan had a savings surplus, a current account surplus, and was, in a sense, independent of world capital markets. If a country is independent of world capital markets, it can set the pace of its own reform, to a certain degree. Second, how long would Marxism have lasted in Russia if the ruble had been convertible? Probably about a week.

East Asia is a capital deficit region, as developing, successful, emergent economies have to be. Capital controls restrict the capital inflows as well as the capital outflows, and these countries need 3–5 percent of GDP in terms of international savings every year. They have to maintain open markets. The secret to being a capital importer is to adopt the rules of international capitalism. If the politicians or the bureaucrats don't make the right decisions, the markets will impose them.

Question: What is the impact on Asia and the global economy of breaking the Hong Kong dollar peg?

Roche: Dreadful. Breaking the peg is not about "face," or Beijing, or handovers, or anything else. It is about the Hong Kong people. In a gross simplification, a Hong Kong balance sheet of the banking system on the asset side has a very big sway of Hong Kong assets. It also has foreign assets, but it has a huge sway of domestic assets associated with real estate. On the liability side, about 12 percent is capital reserves and all the rest is split between foreign and domestic liabilities. A very big proportion of the domestic liabilities are Hong Kong dollars. If the Hong Kong people change those Hong Kong dollar deposits into U.S. dollar deposits, as they can once their time deposits become due, then Hong Kong will run out of foreign exchange reserves overnight. It would, in fact, absorb most of the PRC's foreign exchange reserves as well. Worse than that, if you make a simple assumption that the Hong Kong dollar peg will be broken by the force of people changing their Hong Kong deposit accounts into U.S. dollar accounts and as a result the Hong Kong dollar goes down 20 percent, then 56–66 percent of the capital of Hong Kong banks is gone. The capital is wiped out by the mismatch between the two sides of the balance sheet.

If one financial system is quintessential to the global financial system, it is the Hong Kong banking system. If the Hong Kong banking system were crippled, ramifications would be felt globally. But worse than the financial implications are the political implications. After all, Hong Kong is China's hope to reform and sell off state-owned enterprises. Hong Kong is China's only real capital market for raising the funds it needs to create growth and keep its people reasonably content. If the fundamental health of the Hong Kong banking system is attacked, China's hopes are gone. Therefore, the Hong Kong authorities have absolutely no alternative but to pay the price to maintain the peg until some foreseeable time in the future, which explains why Hong Kong so adamantly defends the peg, both in interest rate terms and verbally, and it is quite right to do so.

If the Hong Kong financial system goes, then what you have seen so far will have been just the first course; the main course is yet to come because the whole of the Asian area and global financial markets will be seriously affected. For that reason, I think the Hong Kong dollar peg will not be allowed to be broken.

Question: Does Asia have the bankruptcy laws in place to get through the necessary financial reforms?

Roche: In many countries, such as Thailand, the answer is no, and it is part and parcel of the reform. In most of the countries, particularly Thailand, Indonesia, and Korea, if a company goes bankrupt and is big enough, the government will take over the company.

Question: How serious is the strain on the Chinese financial system of the overinvestment by the state-owned enterprises?

Roche: The strain is not very serious for the banking system, but it is a serious issue in terms of whether China can absorb the labor force without social unrest.

On the banking side, if one assumes the state-owned enterprises are corporatized properly and then reformed so that the losses stop, China will be left with bad debts worth between 11 and 14 percent of GDP principally in four state-owned banks, which sounds like an awful lot in an economy with a low rate of monetization. But once the losses have been stopped, then those debts could be taken over by the central government, which would raise Chinese public debt-to-GDP ratios to between 35 and 40 percent. So, China would still qualify under the Maastricht criteria for membership in EMU.

Likewise, bad debts are a serious problem, but they will not bring down the economy. China can wrap its bad debts up in a holding company owned by the state, finance the holding company with perpetual government bonds that are never monetized and hardly ever redeemed, and it won't bring down the economy.

What is much more risky is the fact that for the reform of the banking system to work, losses in the state-owned enterprises have to be eliminated. Eliminating these losses basically means getting rid of one-third of the work force, which means that China has to grow in a sustainable fashion at about 9.5–10 percent. Looking at China's real growth, knocking out all the unwanted inventories and the flimflam that goes on in the statistics, shows that the growth rate is probably about 6 percent. So, for China to grow roughly 10 percent, it needs an enormously productive increase in the use of the 30–40 percent savings rate and a huge step forward in the productivity of the labor force. Whether China can absorb the labor force without creating social unrest is the big question.

Question: What can the East Asian countries do to improve the current account crisis?

Roche: One of the steps that Asia could take to help itself is to decrease the elasticity of imports—decrease the amount of imports needed for the economy to grow 1 percent. If a country needs to import 1.5 percent more imports for every 1 percent of growth in domestic demand, the result is a huge import ratio. For example, Ireland, which has the highest level of foreign direct investment into any emergent economy, has an import elasticity about 30 percent lower than in Asia. I am convinced that a country can achieve growth by importing less and making more products domestically. One simple supply-side reform to help import elasticity and the efficient use of capital in Asia is to make every single public infrastructure contract part of a competitive bid process; in the heart of these contracts lies an enormous inefficiency.

Question: What do you think the prospects are for gold in light of the Asian situation?

Roche: I can give you absolutely no rational reason to buy gold, because if the Swiss are selling it, it must be near the end of the world, at least for gold; however, that is the moment you probably want to buy it. I can't see why all of this turmoil in Asia would create a huge bull market for gold. Sure, if the Asian countries reliquify their economies as if there will be no tomorrows and if inflation comes back in the Western economies, and so on, one could make an inflationary argument for buying gold. But those events are not going to happen. Similarly, if the Hong Kong dollar peg breaks and the renminbi starts to fall dramatically and the world financial system becomes unstable, then gold might be an attractive investment. Am I rushing out and buying gold? No, because I don't think these dreadful events will happen.

Research Techniques in Asian Markets

Robert G. Zielinski, CFA
Head of Asian Sector Research
Jardine Fleming Securities, Limited, Singapore

The amount of analytical research needed for evaluating Asian equities depends on how developed the market is. Major problems with the data—ranging from selecting a discount rate to unreliable corporate disclosures to limited data—affect an analyst's ability to research Asian companies. Effective research requires understanding the company and the industry paradigm in which the company operates and using macroanalysis and quantitative studies.

Asian equity research has a life cycle that parallels the development of an emerging market. As a market matures, the level of difficulty and thoroughness of required research increases while the value added from that research decreases, as measured by commission rates. Thus, commission rates are a good indicator of the life cycle of Asian equity research.

When an Asian market just begins to emerge, the main qualification for becoming an equity analyst is to merely be in that country. Research amounts to little more than visiting a company, finding out what products it makes, and then informing investors of this fact (e.g., "Sony makes TVs"). Judging by the high commission rates that can be earned in this stage of development, the value added from these simple activities is high. Life is easy.

Later, as the market truly emerges, commission rates begin to fall, and becoming an analyst requires not only being in the country but also having a brain. Research becomes a little harder; analysts now must compile thick books containing the key facts and figures of listed companies. In the rapid growth phase, further downward pressure is exerted on commissions and further upward pressure on analyst qualifications. At this phase, an M.B.A. is required, and an analyst spends his or her time writing industry notes. Analysis is more detailed and serious than before.

Once the market matures, to get a job as an analyst, previous experience as an analyst is needed, along with the aforementioned qualifications of being in the market, having a brain, and holding an M.B.A. degree. As Asian markets mature, commissions continue to decline; writing about companies and industries adds limited value, and the focus of work becomes thematic research reports, full of original, thought-provoking ideas.

When the market starts to decline, an analyst's qualifications become even tougher; the analyst needs to be a CFA charterholder. Despite all the analyst's knowledge and qualifications, he or she no longer writes research reports because client contacts are the key to earning commissions. In the final stage of development, when the commission rate approaches zero, the job of an analyst is to get the corporate finance deal.

Once a market passes the "just emerging" phase, research becomes the prominent part of an analyst's job. Judging by the direction of commission rates over the past five years, all Asian equity markets have left the emerging stage and are now somewhere in the rapid growth, maturing, or declining stages. This presentation points out some of the important problems in conducting effective research on Asian equities and then explains three phases of research: microanalysis, macroanalysis, and quantitative studies.

Problems

Equity research in Asia has its share of problems. The basic problem is that corporate disclosure is late and unreliable, and the companies are very simple. Only so much can be said about a prawn farmer. In addition, industry data are very rare, and the history of Asian companies is short: A 20-year track record does not exist for a company that was founded last week. The greatest difficulty is the number of different economies and interest rates in this region of the world. Analysts in the United States—where earnings growth is key—have to deal with only one economy and one discount rate, which allows them to make valuation comparisons purely on the basis of relative growth. This simplicity makes U.S. research easy compared with research in Asia. In Asia, both growth and interest rates have to be factored into valuation comparisons. But by the same token, the value added from Asian equity research is much higher than that from U.S. equity research because the rewards for effective research can be significant.

Microanalysis

The first stage of research is microanalysis, which can be divided into company and industry analysis. Knowing that a company actually produces and sells a product and understanding the industry paradigm provide important insights about a company's value.

Company Analysis. The most basic level of research is company analysis, which usually requires a plant visit. As a potential investor, you need to make sure that the company in which you want to invest actually does what it says it does. When I was in Thailand, a lot of controversy surrounded NTS Steel, which was a company that I covered. The company had built a brand-new steel plant equipped with all the latest technology for electric arc furnaces, but investors were concerned that it was not working properly, so I drove out to the steel plant to make sure everything was in order.

Inside the plant, the electric arc furnace was working and producing steel. Then, unfortunately, on the way out, I saw the mountain of inventory. NTS was producing steel, but it was not selling any. When I visited the factory, the stock was at about 100 baht; it is down to about 2 baht now. The inventory problem did not show up in the company's numbers; the only way I learned about it was from the plant visit.

Industry Analysis. When conducting industry analysis, understanding the standard paradigm for that industry is crucial. For example, my rather cynical paradigm for the typical real estate development company in Asia is as follows: A real estate developer is set up and capitalized with a million shares valued at $1 each. So, it has $1 million of net asset value, and it buys a rice paddy for the $1 million. The company is still worth $1 million. Then, the company presells 100 luxury homes at $500,000 each, a 50 percent profit margin. The analysts discount the cash flows based on presales, and the company is suddenly worth $25 million. Next, the company announces a second project. The analysts go back and put the new project into the spreadsheet, discount it, and find that the company is now worth $50 million, at which point it lists and sells a million new shares at $50 each, thus bringing the total net asset value of the company to $100 million. At this time, the main shareholders of the company extract the cash by selling some raw land to the company for $50 million. The value of the company drops to $50 million, and when investors discover that the company never completed its original project, the value soon plummets to zero. This example is a typical entrepreneurship in the Asian real estate industry, and realizing this fact tells the analyst what to pay attention to.

Bangkok Land, which at one time had the world's largest real estate development project, somewhat fits this paradigm. Bangkok Land presold 20,000 condominiums. It recognized the revenues and profits as a percentage of completion, even though the buyers had put down only about 10 percent of the purchase price. To see how things were progressing, I visited the construction site. The condominiums had actually been built, but five years later, no one had moved in. The company's stock price went through three phases. In 1992, when people initially had doubts about the company, the share price fell from around 200 baht to about 60 baht. When the markets took off in 1993, Bangkok Land's stock price went up to about 175 baht; investors were in denial about the problems: Maybe everything would work out. Since then, the sentiment has been one of doom; the price now hovers around 5 baht.

Macroanalysis

Macroanalysis is a little more advanced, as one might expect, than microanalysis. Macroeconomic analysis looks to a country's economy to figure out what is happening within an industry. I have used macroanalysis for about three years to show people what is happening with Asian banks. Asian banks have been financing an economic boom. **Figure 1** shows that the annual loan growth of Asian banks has been tremendous, between 20 percent and 30 percent. These economies have seen a lot of credit expansion, and of course, this borrowed money has not been spent as it might have been in the United States. Americans love to consume, but Asians invest—especially in real estate.

The ratio of investment to total GDP has risen in all of these economies, as shown in **Figure 2**, which generally is viewed as good. But half of all investment has been in the property market, which is not good. A lot of the rest of the money has gone into purchases such as company cars, because anything a company buys is considered investment. So, many of the investments have been rather foolish ones.

As a result, Asian banks have become overexposed to the property market, as shown in **Figure 3**. The Asian economic growth miracle has been fueled

Figure 1. Asian Banks' Loan Growth, 1985–96

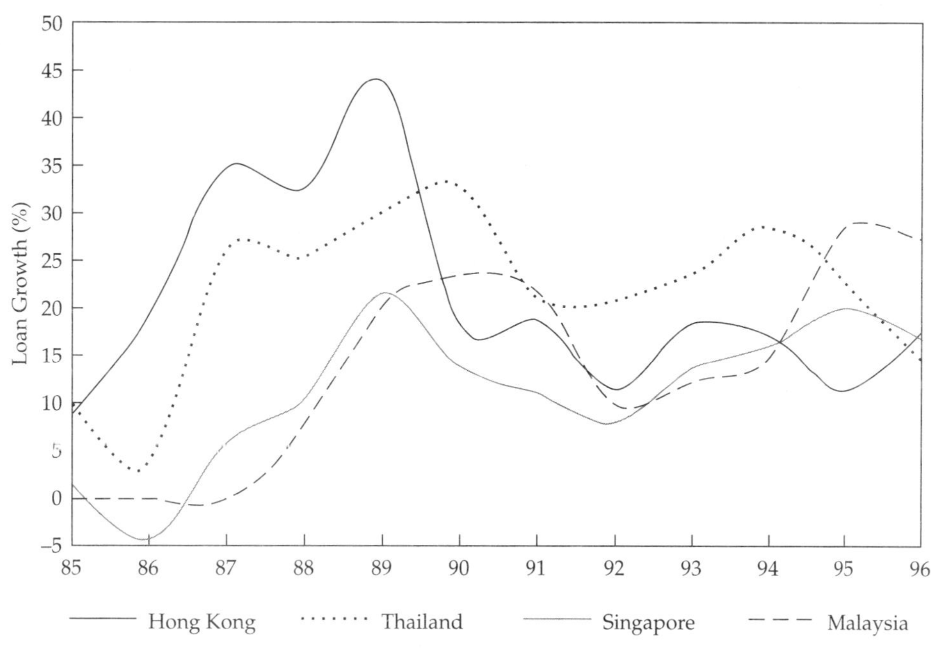

Note: Loan growth is expressed as year-over-year growth.

Figure 2. Gross Fixed Capital Formation (GFCF) to Total GDP for Various Asian Countries, 1985–96

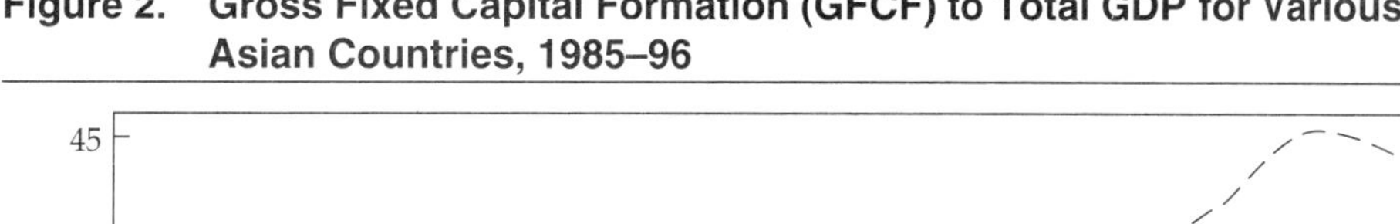

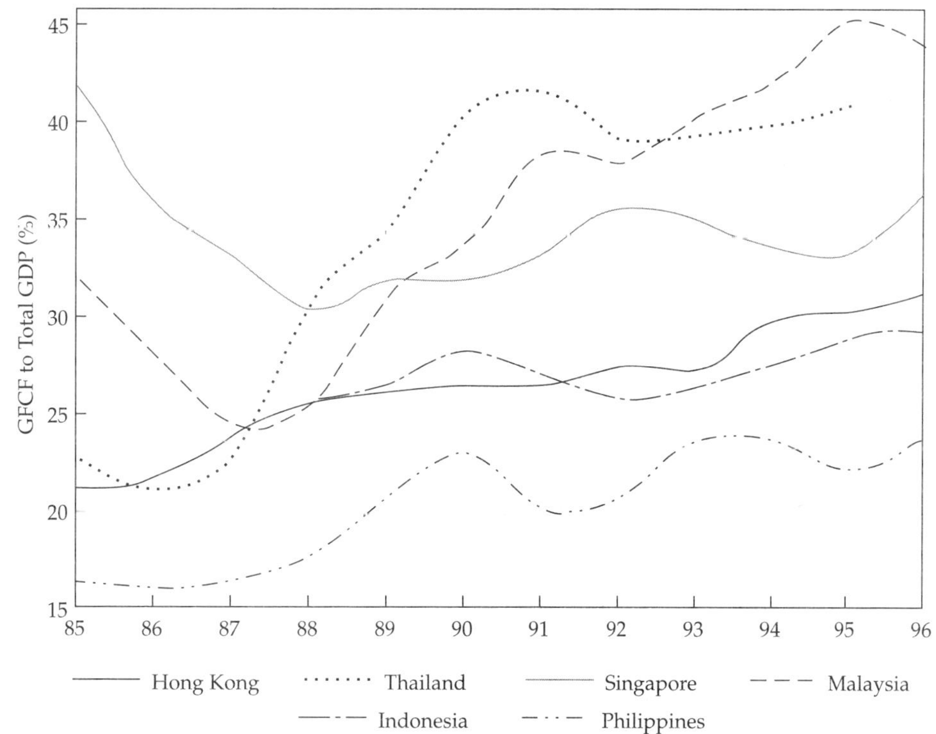

Figure 3. Banks' Exposure to Property: Hong Kong and Singapore

A. Hong Kong Banks

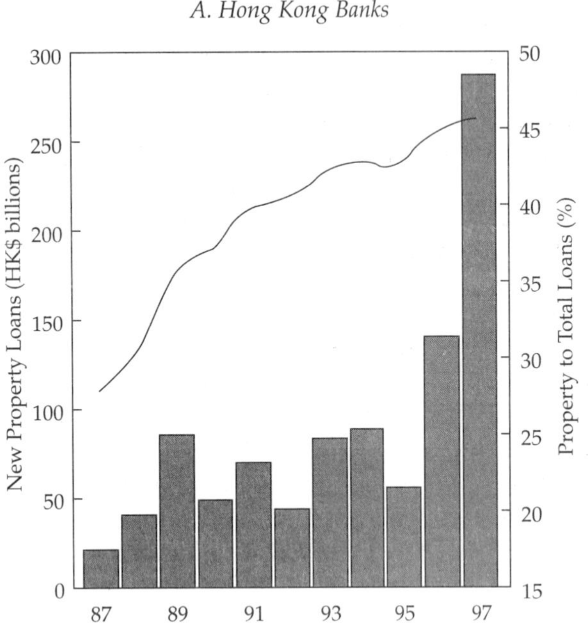

B. Singapore Banks

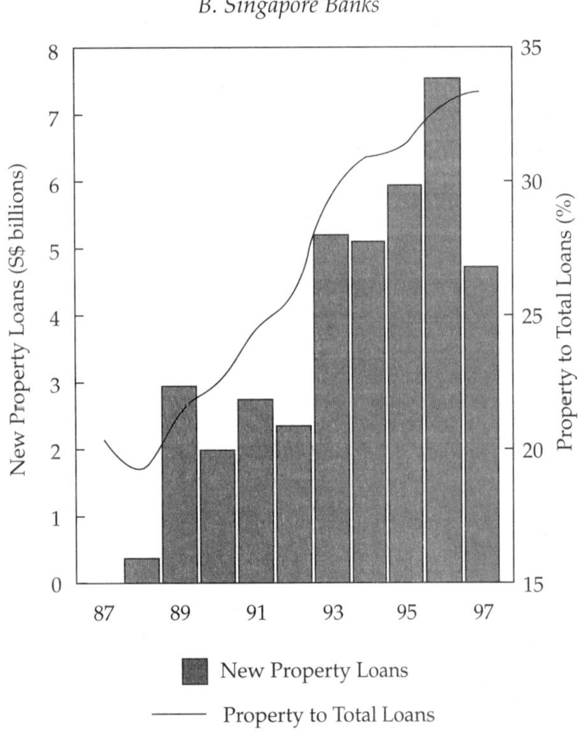

Note: No new property loans were made in Singapore in 1987.

by bank lending in the property market, and when real estate investors spend the money, they get growth. It is a virtual circle that will continue until the banks eventually stop lending to property companies and the game is unfortunately over.

Event Studies. Event studies are one way of conducting macroanalysis. At Jardine Fleming, we used an event study to analyze how a currency devaluation would affect profits in the banking industry, because none of the textbooks told us exactly what devaluation does. We looked at seven cases of devaluation from around the world in the past 15 years and tried to reach conclusions. After the devaluation of the Thai baht in November 1984, the Thai baht exchange rate went from 23 to 28 baht to the U.S. dollar. Spreads collapsed at Thai banks, as shown in Panel A of **Figure 4**. Similarly, the return on equity (ROE) of Thai banks collapsed, as shown in Panel B of Figure 4; ROE was down in 1985 and particularly in 1986. So, based on this event study, the outlook for Asian banks for the 1998–99 period is rotten. People are just starting to recognize that Asian currency devaluations are a bad thing because they drag down the U.S. market, which in turn affects the rest of the world.

Another event study looked at the effect of devaluation on GDP growth. Mexico's GDP growth went from 4 percent to –6 percent after devaluation; roughly the same happened in India—from 5 percent to about zero percent GDP growth. Based on this event study, 1998 looks to be a bad year for GDP growth across Asia.

Cluster Analysis. We have found that the more we analyze the Asian markets, the more we think we can identify three systems of economic development: the nationalists, the capitalists, and the socialists. These three systems can be considered paradigms for understanding the behavior of companies. Banks can be used as an example. The banks in the nationalist countries—Japan, South Korea, Taiwan, and China—do not care about ROE or making a profit. They just want to make loans to petrochemical companies, for instance. The more loans they shovel out the door to heavy industry, the happier they are. The thinner the spread between the cost of capital and the interest rate charged on the loan, the happier they are, because it means greater efficiency for the borrower. When asked about the petrochemical company's ROE, the bank managers do not know the answer. When asked about their own bank's ROE, these bank managers do not know the concept. But when asked about the petrochemical loans, the bank managers get all excited. In a nationalist framework, the banks sacrifice their profits for the good of the industry and basically forget about everything else (e.g., the bank's ROE). The banks are weak, but the companies are strong.

Figure 4. Thailand Devaluation Effects: Spreads and Return on Equity, 1984–93

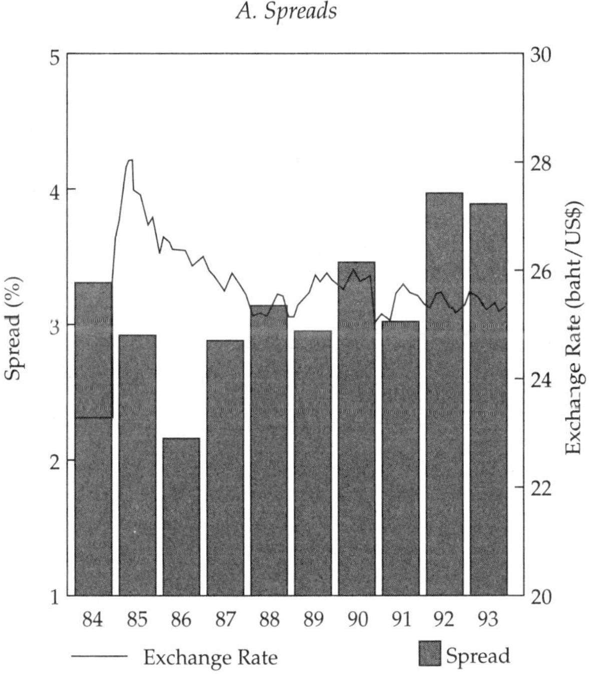

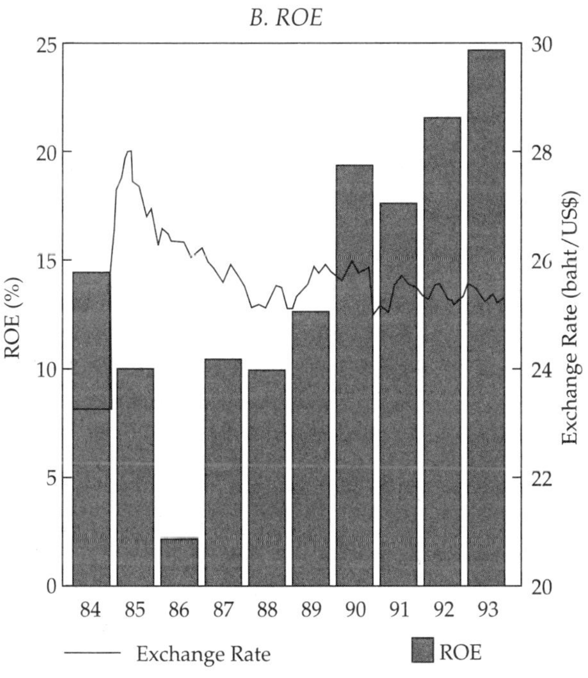

The Asian capitalist countries are Hong Kong, Singapore, Thailand, Malaysia, and the Philippines. The banks in these countries are dominated by Chinese owners, and what they care about is family wealth. Spreads are fat because these banks overcharge their borrowers and avoid costly competition by setting up cartels. These are, or used to be, the most profitable banks in the entire world. All their lending tends to be quite short term—for items such as trade finance or get-rich-quick property. In the capitalist system, banks are extremely strong—or were until recently—but heavy industry loans are virtually nonexistent, which explains why these countries do not have much of an industrial base.

The socialist countries, such as Sri Lanka, India, Pakistan, and Indonesia, nationalized their banking industry to drive out the British, Dutch, and other nondomestic banks and then forced the banks to expand throughout the rural areas. This policy was to correct a social ill. Until the arrival of banks in rural areas, a local farmer was totally dependent on local money lenders in times of need. For example, if a farmer's wife needed an operation, he would have to borrow at exorbitant rates of interest and pledge his farm as collateral. Even if his wife recovered, the farmer would be unable to repay the loan; he would then lose his land and become a serf. Unfortunately, the farmers do not repay the nationalized banks any better than they did the money lenders, so nonperforming loans have been a problem. The result is a weak banking system and weak industry.

Impact Assessment. Impact assessment is another research technique that we commonly use to quantify the size of opportunities or problems. For example, one of the big issues facing banks today is the extent of the nonperforming loan (NPL) situation. No one knows for sure quite how bad the situation will become. We conducted an impact assessment to estimate how high NPLs would be for each sector of bank lending, as shown in **Table 1**. In Thailand, we think 50 percent of property loans will become nonperforming. In Indonesia, maybe 25 percent of property loans will be nonperforming. Loans to the electric utilities, as well as loans to agriculture, should be okay for all these countries. For personal loans, we guess 15–20 percent will be nonperforming. We looked at all the numbers and estimated that the total NPLs (as a percentage of all outstanding loans) run anywhere between 13 percent for the Philippines to 19 percent for Thailand. Actually, we believe that the level of NPLs in Southeast Asia will be greater than in Japan.

Continuing that same analysis, we found that as a percentage of GDP, the country hardest hit by NPLs is actually Malaysia, because it has so much credit outstanding. As **Figure 5** shows, Malaysia and Thailand look very vulnerable. Singapore is somewhat of a "safe haven," as is the Philippines; the Philippines has not had as much time to lend to the property developers as its healthier neighbors have.

Table 1. Estimated Peak NPLs by Sector and for All Outstanding Loans (percent of total loans)

Loan Sector	Indonesia	Malaysia	Philippines	Thailand
Agriculture	10%	0%	10%	10%
Manufacturing	15	8	12	20
Electricity	0	0	0	0
Property	25	20	20	50
Trade	12	20	5	5
Financial	25	20	25	20
Personal	15	15	12	20
All Loans	17	16	13	19

Figure 5. Peak Nonperforming Loans as a Percentage of GDP for Various Asian Countries

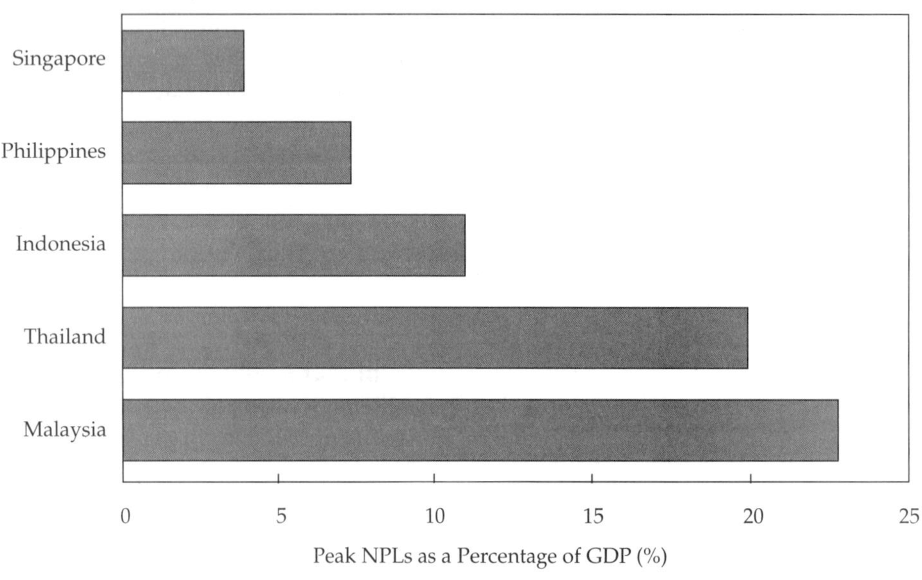

Quantitative Studies

Quantitative studies involve conducting empirical studies and creating valuation models.

Empirical Studies. Economic value added (EVA) is the buzzword on Wall Street these days. EVA is basically the ROE minus the cost of equity (COE) multiplied by shareholders' equity; that calculation yields the value added for the year. We use a simpler approach: We have found that the interbank rate is a perfect proxy for COE. **Figure 6** shows the relationship between various Asian banks' price-to-book ratios (P/Bs) and the difference between their ROEs and the interbank rate. The magic formula that we derived from this analysis for valuing a bank is

$$P/B = 1.1 + 0.14 \times (\text{ROE} - \text{Interbank rate}).$$

Another, more advanced study that we completed analyzed the returns of bank stocks versus beta. As **Figure 7** shows, beta does not work in Asia, just like it does not work in the United States. Bank stock returns are unrelated to the beta of the stock. They are, however, related to the P/B of the bank. We found that by buying Asian bank stocks with the lowest P/Bs and holding them for a year, we could earn 40 percent. Of course, this analysis is based on 1990–96 data, when the banks were doing well. The top quintile of P/B banks returned nothing, which has been demonstrated in 1997: The Philippine and Malaysian banks had no problems up until devaluation; however, they have fallen as much as the Thai banks have. Thus, high P/B stocks are dangerous in Asia.

Valuation Models. Valuation models, such as the dividend discount model (DDM), are the most advanced technique for conducting quantitative analysis. One of the difficulties of using the DDM in Asian emerging markets is choosing an appropriate discount rate. Because no long-term government

Figure 6. P/B versus ROE Less Interbank Rate for Various Asian Banks

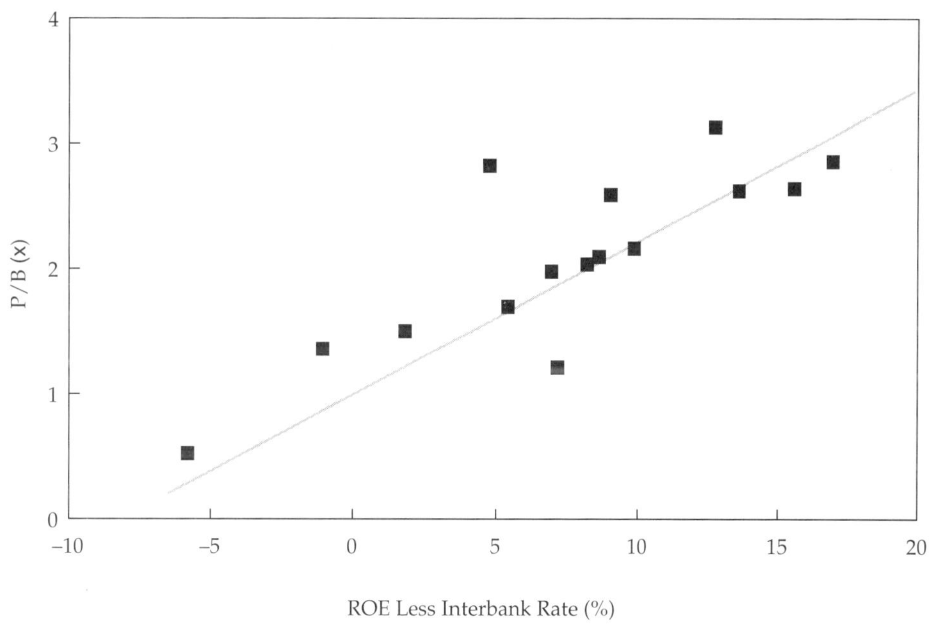

bond yields exist in Asian emerging markets for determining a risk-free rate of interest, we have to calculate a synthetic one based on U.S. real rates, local interest rates, and the local inflation rate. For example, this technique yields a cost of capital with the embedded risk premium for Asian banks ranging from about 8 percent in Japan to about 23 percent for Pakistan and Sri Lanka. In DDMs, the emphasis is on interest rates and earnings. Malaysian bank price-to-book ratios perfectly track what the DDM says they should, based on their ROEs and COEs. The same has been true, until recently, for Hong Kong banks, which proves that Asian equity markets are not speculative casinos, unless one is speculating about fundamentals. The Korean banks, shown in **Figure 8**, were very stubborn. Their valuations had remained well above what the DDM had indicated for seven years, but finally, valuations have matched what we said they should, about half of book value. Our biggest difficulties occur in countries in which interest rates are very high, such as Indonesia, where we cannot accurately model bank valuations.

Another technique is to look at the multiple of enterprise value (EV) to earnings before interest, taxes, depreciation, and amortization (EBITDA). We have found this ratio to be very useful in making cross-border comparisons. As **Table 2** shows, on the basis of price to cash flow, Korean Air looks cheap, 1.5 times, compared with Cathay Pacific, 7.7 times. But once the debt is added into the market value of the equity, the EV/EBITDA multiple shows a different story. Korean Air has $1 billion of market value and $6 billion of debt. Looking at EV/EBITDA shows that Korean Air is the more expensive company.

A third valuation technique, which I developed specifically for banks, is "fin value" to EBPATA (earnings before provisions after tax adjusted for NPLs). It was designed to address one of the most important issues in Asian banking: how to value banks with high levels of NPLs. **Figure 9** illustrates what rising NPLs can do to a bank's net income and ROE over time. During those periods when NPLs are rising rapidly, such traditional valuation measures as P/E, P/B, or ROE tend to break down—earnings are distorted and the book value is suspect. NPLs have been fluctuating wildly in Asia, ranging from 33 percent of the total loans outstanding in Malaysia in 1989 to about 5 percent or 6 percent; recently they have been heading up to 15 percent.

Table 2. EV/EBITDA: Airline Industry

Item	Korean Air	Cathay Pacific
Financial data		
Number of Boeing 747s	40	32
Revenue passenger kilometers (millions)	33,513	35,323
Market value (US$ million)	966	5,491
Price/cash flow (×)	1.5	7.7
Debt (US$ million)	5,653	455
Analytical values		
EV (US$ million)	6,619	5,946
EBITDA (US$ million)	959	991
EV/EBITDA (×)	6.9	6.0

Figure 7. Asian Bank Stock Returns versus Beta and P/B, 1990–96

A. Return as a Function of Beta

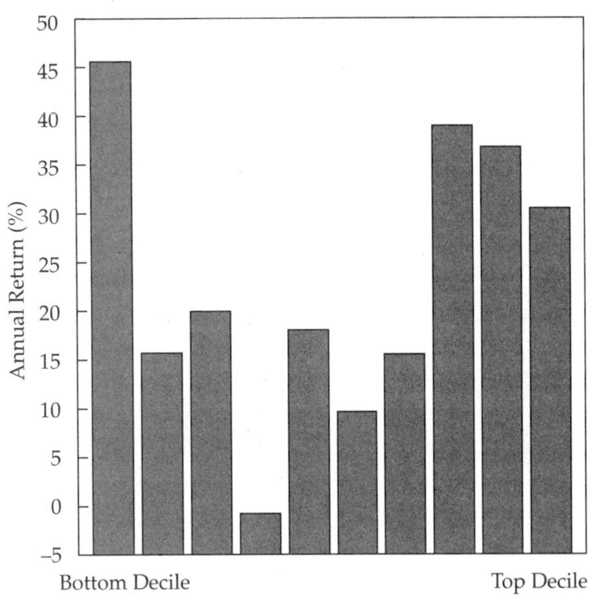

B. Return as a Function of P/B

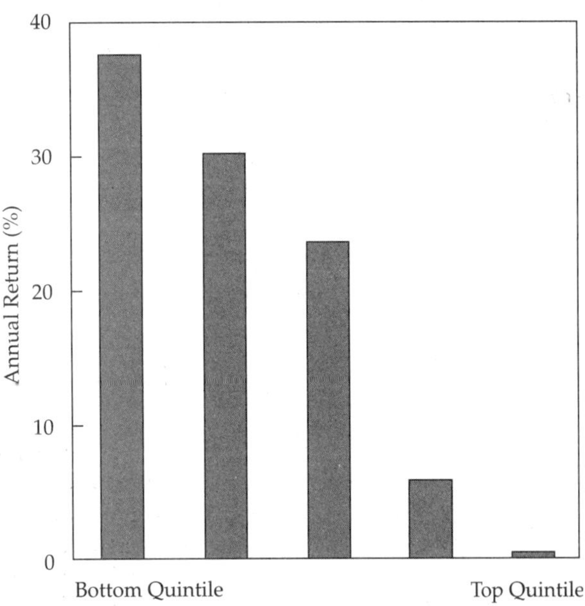

When valuing such a bank, the solution to accounting for NPLs is fin value. That is, the value of a bank is equal to the market value of its equity plus the value of its NPLs after tax, which is the equivalent to enterprise value in an industrial company, where debt is added to the market value of equity. The theory is that if a clean bank is valued at $100, then an investor would be willing to pay only $60 for a similar bank that had $40 in NPLs. Thus, the total value (fin value) of a bank is the sum of its market value plus NPLs, or equivalently, the value of a bank with NPLs is equal to its value if it were clean less the amount of NPLs. The cash flow to fin value, just like EBITDA to enterprise value, is the bank's net income plus annual loan loss provisions and the interest income not received on its NPLs. This cash flow is EBPATA, and it is the cash flow a bank would generate if it had no NPLs.

We find that this ratio of fin value to EBPATA can be reduced to two extreme cases: Scenario 1, where a bank has no NPLs and no provisions, and Scenario 2, where a bank has so many NPLs that its market value falls to zero and it generates no income to make provisions, pay taxes, or report profits. The following equations simplify the ratio of fin value to EBPATA for each extreme:

$$\text{Scenario 1} = \frac{\text{Market value}}{\text{Net income}} = \text{P/E}$$

$$\text{Scenario 2} = \frac{\text{Fin value}}{\text{EBPATA}} = \frac{\text{NPL} \times (1-t)}{\text{NPL} \times \text{Lending rate} \times (1-t)} = \frac{1}{\text{Lending rate}}.$$

Thus, the fin value to EBPATA ratio is neutral to NPLs. For a bank with no NPLs or provisions, the fin value/EBPATA multiple reduces to P/E. If the whole value of the bank is in the form of NPLs, fin value/EBPATA reduces to 1 divided by the lending rate. This ratio gives us an indication as to what the appropriate fin value/EBPATA ratio should be: approximately one divided by the local lending rate, a number that tends to be close to the P/Es in Asian emerging markets.

The ratio of fin value to EBPATA for most Asian markets is merely the inverse of interest rates, which is a startling revelation because it means that valuing a bank is easy: Calculate the market value of the bank by looking at the cash flow it would generate if it were clean, multiply it by the inverse of interest rates, and then subtract the after-tax value of the bank's NPLs. **Figure 10** illustrates how this approach allows analysts to look at the P/B of Thailand's Bangkok Bank as a function of its NPLs. The two lines represent the P/B under two interest rate scenarios: 1993's low interest rates and those in 1996. If Bangkok Bank had no NPLs in 1996, its P/B would be about 1.5 times. But at 13 percent NPLs, the appropriate P/B would be 1.0 times, and at 27 percent NPLs, the appropriate P/B would be 0.5 times. Thus, this model makes NPLs explicit, rather than implicit as the DDM would.

Figure 8. DDM Valuations: Korean Banks, January 1990–March 1997

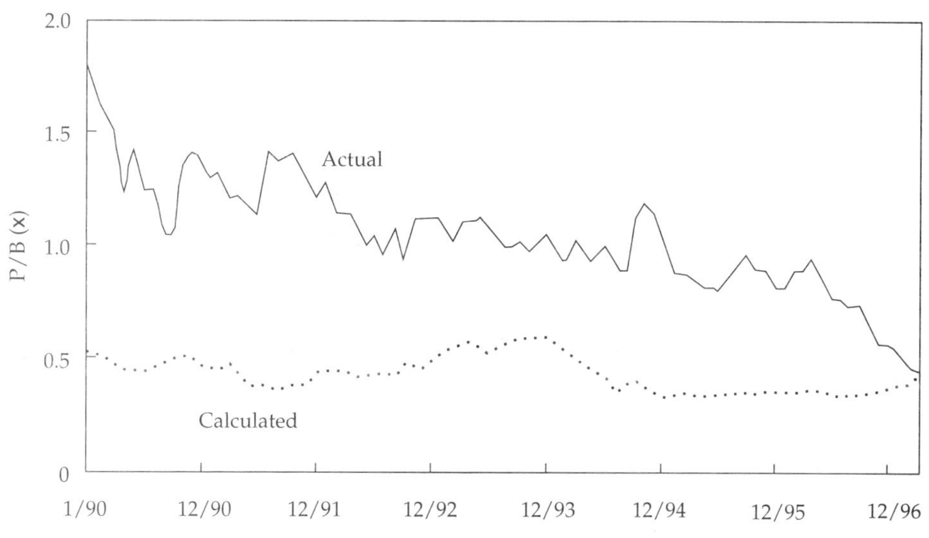

Figure 9. The Relationship of Bank Net Income and ROE to NPLs/Total Loans

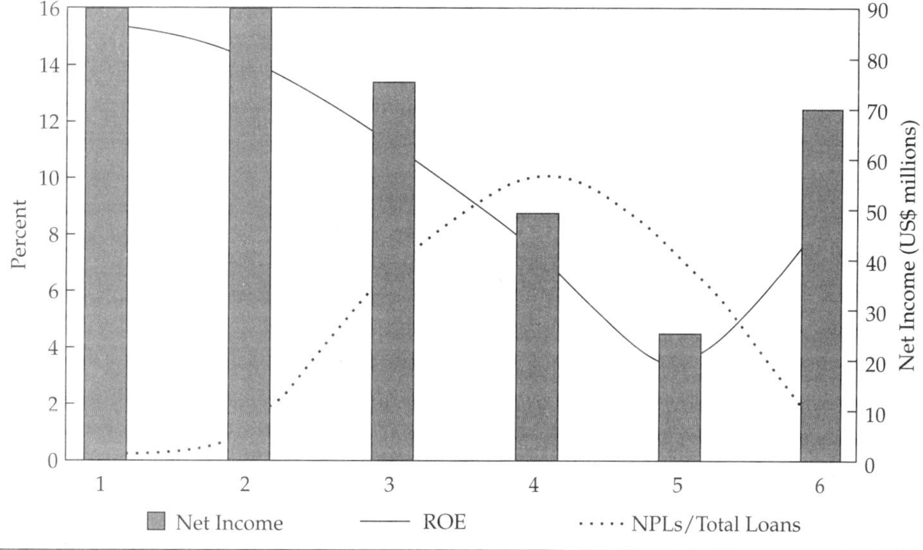

Conclusion

Analytical research on Asian markets presents analysts with interesting challenges, but potentially high returns are the reward for effective research. Lack of reliable disclosures from firms and insufficient industry data prompt the analyst to use other research techniques.

Conducting company visits and understanding the industry paradigm in which a firm operates provide insight into valuing a company and help identify problems. Macroanalysis, which examines a country's economy, helps identify cyclical and secular trends that affect industry growth and company valuations. For example, event studies, cluster analysis, and impact assessments clearly provide insight into the outlook for Asian bank stocks.

Quantitative analysis takes research techniques to the next level. Empirical studies on EVA and enterprise value are more challenging to complete but are very helpful for performing relative valuations of companies within the same industry. Dividend discount models and proprietary valuation models provide additional quantitative analysis, but selecting the appropriate discount rate—a key parameter for these models—is difficult in Asian countries because there are so many different interest rates for different countries and risk premiums for different industries. These models also break down in certain industries. For example, they do not work in the banking industry because nonperforming loans wipe out earnings. Another model, such as fin value to EBPATA, which is neutral to nonperforming loans, is needed.

Figure 10. P/B versus NPLs as a Percentage of Total Loans for Bangkok Bank

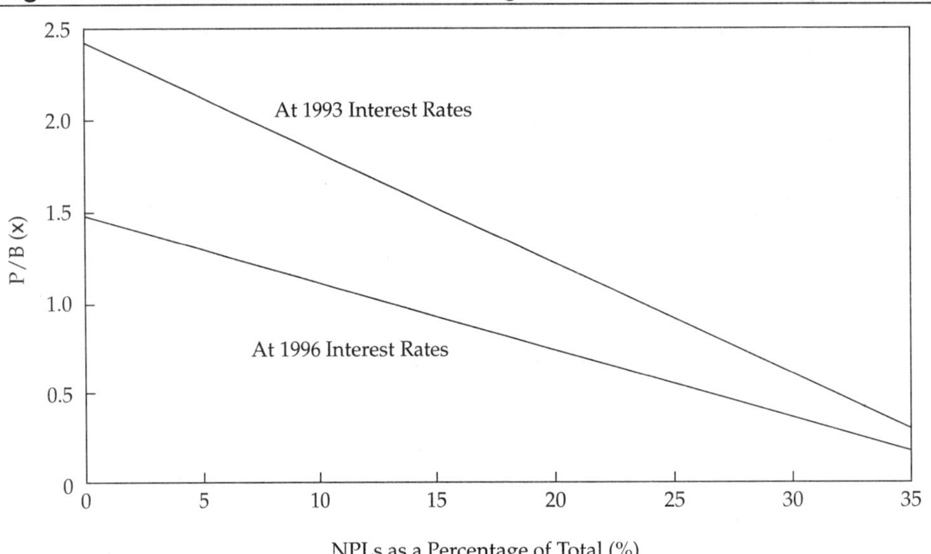

Equity Style Investing

Richard Bernstein
First Vice President, Director, Quantitative and Equity Derivatives Research
Merrill Lynch & Company

Nigel Tupper
Vice President
Merrill Lynch & Company, Singapore

Style investing is more than simply value and growth investing; it is an investment scheme that groups stocks based on common characteristics. Influenced by structural, psychological, and informational asymmetries within the market, equity styles do not perform consistently over time because of changes in profit, credit, and interest rate cycles. Understanding these factors and the earnings expectation life cycle is the key to successful investing. The Asia Pacific region provides good examples of how styles work differently around the world and illustrates when certain styles are most successful.

Factors that influence style investing are consistent around the world. Of course, all economies may not be in sync, so investors may get different signals from different markets. Therefore, knowing how to read these signals is critical for the international investor.

This presentation provides a clear definition of equity style investing, explains how structural, psychological, and informational asymmetries influence the relative performance of alternative equity styles, and discusses the importance of three factors that affect style rotation: profits, credit, and interest rates. In addition, the earnings expectation life cycle provides useful insight into successful investing, helps differentiate good managers from bad managers, and shows the relative value added of tactical versus strategic allocation. Finally, Australia, Hong Kong, Malaysia, and Singapore provide good examples of how styles tend to change around the world and when certain styles outperform or underperform.

Definition of Equity Styles

All too often people use simplistic definitions of equity styles, for example, referring only to value versus growth.[1] At Merrill Lynch, we prefer to define an equity style as a market segment with common characteristics that tend to perform as a group over several economic and market cycles. By this definition, a style could be based on a bottom-up approach, such as looking for stocks with low P/Es, or on a top-down approach, such as focusing on a particular industry. Many people think that the top-down approach starts with macroeconomic analysis and extends down to individual industries and companies, but it is also a type of investment style.

Styles exist because all stocks do not perform similarly; their relative performance can be explained by structural, psychological, and informational asymmetries (or segments) within the market.

- *Structural.* Structural segments of the market are created when managers (or their clients) restrict the investable universe. Various factors contribute to the creation of structural segments in the market, including investment charters or mandates, permissible investments, and a manager's (or client's) degree of risk tolerance. When managers promote themselves as particular types of managers, they create structural boundaries that prevent them from investing in certain parts of the market. Managers are also limited by structural boundaries that restrict their international investments to "investable" stocks, but the definition of investable varies widely around the world. The existence of barriers to investment creates opportunities and is one of the reasons styles exist.

[1]For further reading on style investing, see Richard Bernstein, *Style Investing: Unique Insight into Equity Management* (New York: John Wiley & Sons, 1995).

Psychological. Psychological segments of the market are created because of psychological biases that all people have. An example of a psychological bias is regret aversion. Meir Statman, a pioneering researcher in the field of behavioral finance, describes regret aversion as a manager's having to tell a client that he or she is sorry. Suppose the manager buys a stock from a company with a good reputation, but the stock price goes down. The manager can report to the client that it was a great company but the company's management made a mistake. The manager can say: "At our firm, we know the company and are confident that it will do better in the future." In this case, the manager is not at fault, the company is—in the manager's mind and in the client's mind. Take another example: a junky company that the manager thinks will turn around. If the company does not perform, the client might turn to the manager and say, "You are an idiot. Who in their right mind would buy the worst company in the industry?" The manager ends up having to tell the client that he or she is sorry, which is extremely unpleasant. Regret aversion typically causes investors (and managers) to look for good companies, not good stocks.

Psychological factors may be one of the biggest contributors to market segments and to the existence of equity styles.

Information asymmetry. Information asymmetry is a fancy way of saying that not all companies have the same flow of information. Almost every day an analyst can find a piece of information about IBM Corporation by looking on Bloomberg. For a smaller company, such as Charming Shoppes, an analyst might be lucky to find one piece of information a month; more than likely, the analyst can get only the quarterly earnings release. Likewise, the number of analysts following each of these companies is likely to be quite different. When the number of analysts following a stock is out of sync with what is appropriate, the stock price can be affected—either positively or negatively. For example, at one time, more analysts were following Ascend Communications, which has a market capitalization of $7 billion, than General Electric Company, which has a market capitalization of $251 billion. The stock price for Ascend Communications rose too high and is now imploding. In this case, there was an asymmetry in the flow of information.

Style Rotation

Styles do not consistently perform; they rotate in cycles. Investors need to pay attention to style rotation even if they are "disciplined" investors.

Good companies do not necessarily make good stock investments over the long term. Investors often say that portfolio managers have to buy stocks from good companies: The stocks from good companies are the crux of any portfolio strategy because they outperform in the long run. This assertion is not true in the United States. **Figure 1** shows the 12-year performance for an index of the best-rated stocks versus

Figure 1. A+ versus C and D Rated Stocks, February 1986–September 1997

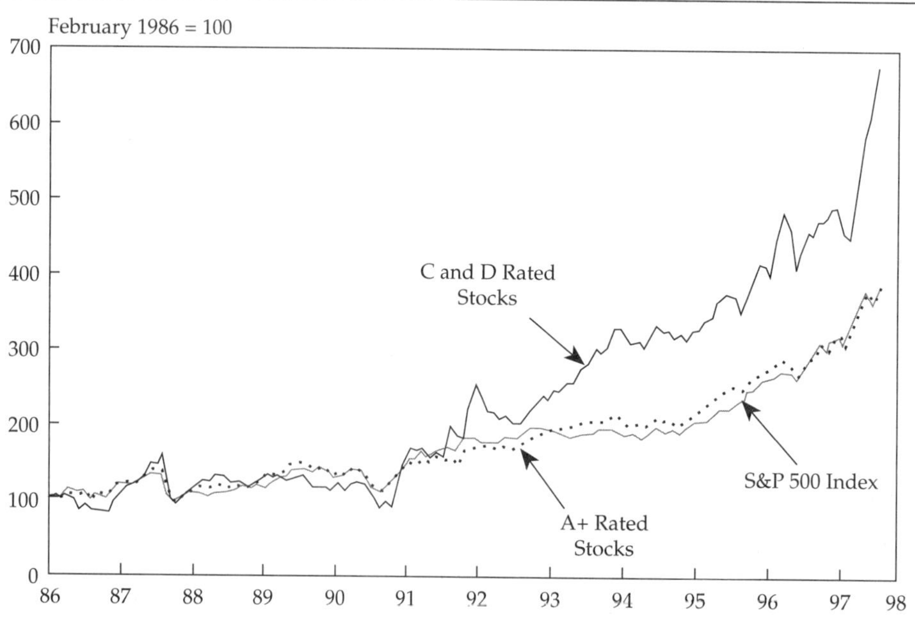

Note: Stocks are categorized by their S&P Common Stock Ratings. Portfolios are equal weighted and rebalanced monthly.

an index of the worst-rated stocks. The stocks are grouped based on their Standard & Poor's Corporation Common Stock Rating. In the rating scheme, a stable growth company would rate "A+", and a bankrupt company would rate "D". As can be seen in Figure 1, the index of C and D rated stocks outperformed both the A+ stocks and the S&P 500 Index.

Good companies do not make good stocks over the long term for several reasons. First, a diversified portfolio of large-capitalization, high-quality stocks is essentially the market—or an expensive index fund. In contrast, the lower-rated companies are often completely ignored, but over the time period shown in Figure 1, they almost doubled the performance of the A+ rated companies.

Successful long-term strategies may also experience periods during which they underperform in the short term. **Figure 2** shows the relative performance of a high earnings yield (i.e., low P/E) strategy in the United States—in general, a strategy that has worked well in the United States since 1986. Despite the fact that it has worked well in the long term, significant periods of underperformance can be seen in Figure 2. For example, in 1990, the relative underperformance was so bad that many value managers were fired because their clients did not want to "ride out the storm." Unfortunately, some of these managers were forced out of business by the double whammy of declining asset values and the outflow of funds. The decision that "I am a long-term investor, and I am going to follow one discipline" may, at times, be a poor business decision.

Given the significance of these cycles, one can see the importance of understanding what factors affect style rotation. Three key factors affecting style rotation are profits, credit, and interest rates.

Profits. At Merrill Lynch, our work shows that by far the most important factor influencing style rotation is the profit cycle. The profit cycle rule works in every major market around the world. The cycles of style rotation are based primarily on the abundance, or scarcity, of reported profit growth. **Figure 3** shows the relative performance of growth versus value styles (based on a sample of mutual funds) plotted against a measure of EPS momentum for the S&P 500. Earnings momentum is defined as the year-over-year percentage change in S&P 500 reported earnings on a trailing four-quarter basis. Note that we use reported earnings, not earnings before interest, taxes, depreciation, and amortization (EBITDA) or enterprise value.

The pattern is fairly consistent. When the profit cycle peaks and starts to decelerate, growth managers outperform value managers. The explanation, we believe, is that as earnings become scarce, investors bid up the price of that scarce resource and multiples expand on a smaller and smaller number of companies

Figure 2. Top 50 S&P 500 Companies by Earnings Yield, January 1986–September 1997

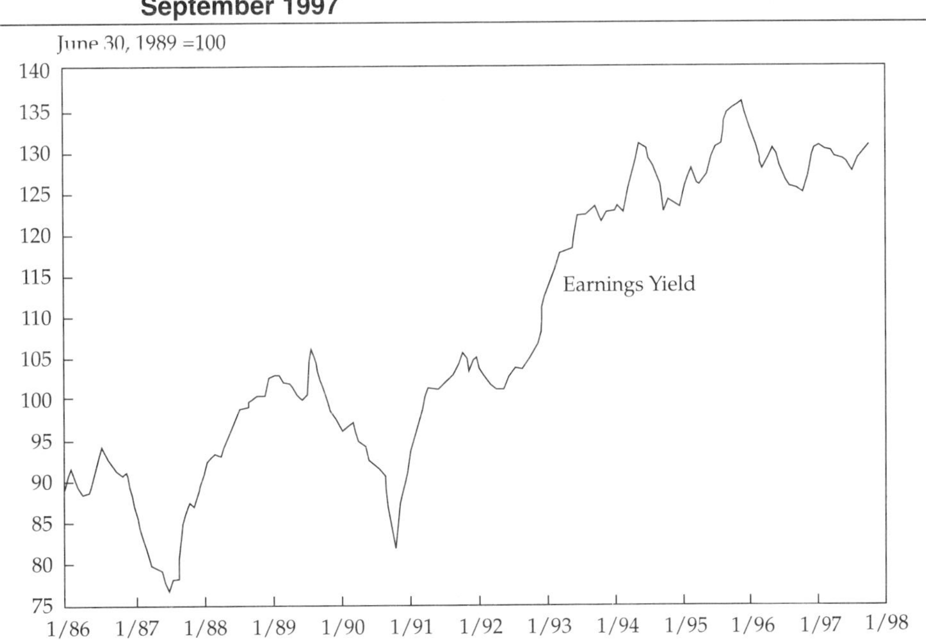

Note: Performance data are calculated as the relative cumulative performance versus an equal-weighted S&P 500 Index.

Figure 3. Growth versus Value: Relative Performance and S&P 500 EPS Momentum, January 1970–September 1997

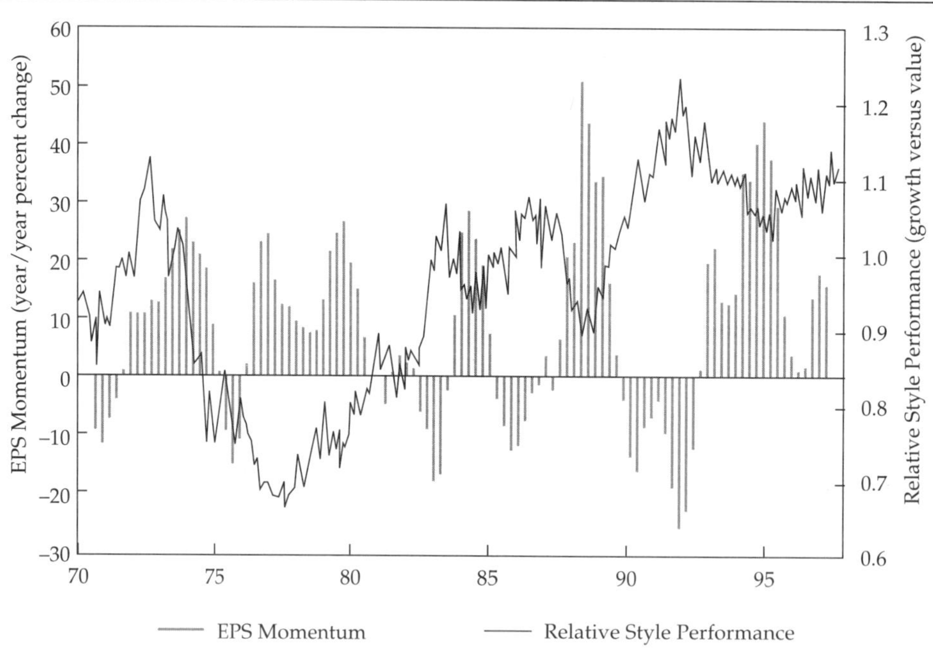

Note: EPS momentum is calculated as the year/year percent change in the S&P 500 four quarters EPS figures. Style performance is based on Merrill Lynch Quantitative Analysis' growth fund index versus value fund index.

that can maintain their growth rates. When the profit cycle begins to trough and then accelerate, value managers outperform growth managers. The explanation is that as earnings growth becomes more abundant, investors become selective shoppers: They look for comparatively cheap stocks and bid up the prices of those cheap stocks.

Credit. The performance of growth and value funds is also related to the credit cycle. **Figure 4** shows the relationship between the performance of growth and value funds and the credit cycle, measured by Moody's Investors Service's default rate. Quite simply, as the default rate goes up, growth funds tend to outperform value funds. As the default rate goes down, value tends to outperform growth. The correlation is reasonably tight (ρ greater than 90 percent during the 1990s), and the relationship is logical. As the default rate increases, investors want to be invested in the good companies. **Figure 5** clearly illustrates the tight relationship between stock quality performance and credit spreads over time.

The 1970s provide a good example of the outperformance of value, low quality, and small stocks. Small stocks in the United States had one of their biggest runs during the 1970s—a period of inflation. Correlations between the quality considerations in the stock market and the quality considerations in the bond market were very tight. With the inflationary spiral during that time period, nominal growth accelerated, which was good for value investing, low-quality investing, and small-stock investing. People forget that small stocks work well during periods of inflation.

Interest Rates. Finally, style rotation is also related to interest rates. **Figure 6** shows that growth funds outperform value funds in periods of declining and low interest rates and that value outperforms growth in periods of rising and high interest rates. Stocks with longer durations tend to be more interest rate sensitive than stocks with shorter durations. The basic theme is that growth is a longer-duration strategy than value. The easy way to think about that statement is that growth stocks usually have high P/Es and low dividend yields. The high P/E means that a firm discounts events far into the future, and the low yield means that the firm's interim cash flow is relatively low. Conversely, value stocks, which tend to have low P/Es, imply that a firm's time horizon is short, and its high dividend yield means that the interim cash flow in that short time horizon is high.

Earnings Expectations Life Cycle

Expectations play a major role in assessing whether a company sells at an attractive price. **Figure 7** shows

Figure 4. Moody's Investors Service Default Rate and Growth and Value Fund Performance, 1975–97

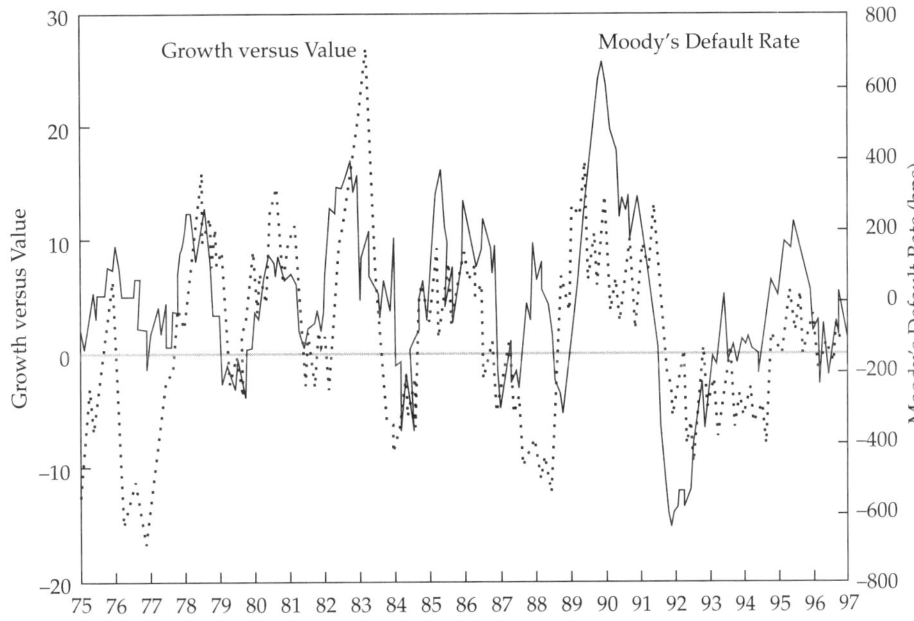

Growth versus Value
Moody's Default Rate
Growth versus Value
Moody's Default Rate (bps)
30
20
10
0
−10
−20
800
600
400
200
0
−200
−400
−600
−800
75 76 77 78 79 80 81 82 83 84 85 86 87 88 89 90 91 92 93 94 95 96 97

Note: The growth versus value comparison is based on 12-month relative performance. Moody's default rate is the 12-month difference in basis points.

Source: Based on data from Moody's Investors Service.

Figure 5. Stock Quality and Credit Spreads, January 1986–September 1997

Stock Quality
Credit Spread
Stock Quality (relative price)
Credit Quality Spread (bps)
1.4
1.2
1.0
0.8
0.6
0.4
1000
900
800
700
600
500
400
300
200
100
86 87 88 89 90 91 92 93 94 95 96 97 98

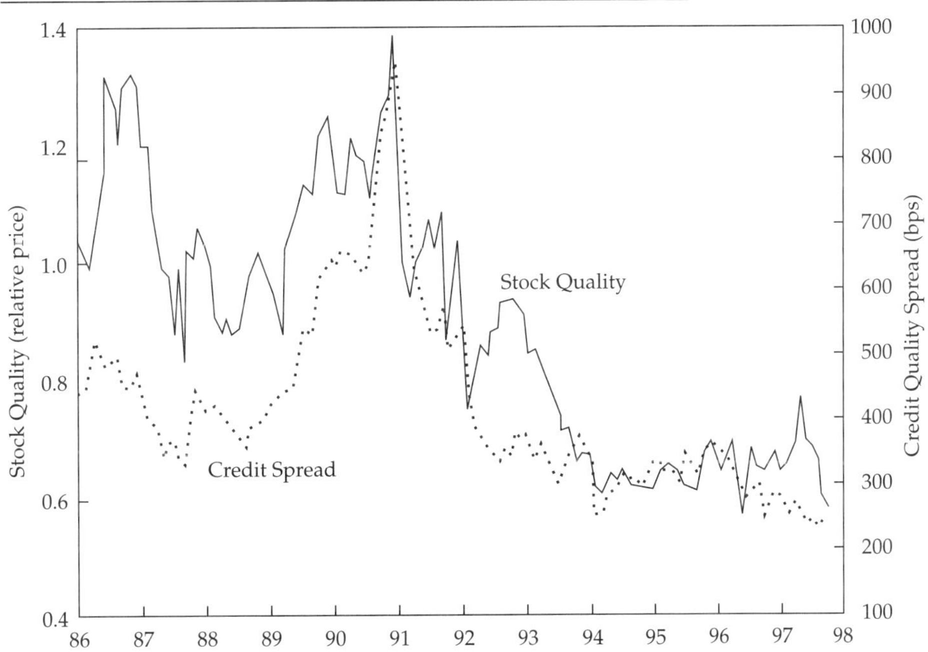

Note: Stock quality is represented by the relative price performance of A+ versus C and D rated stocks. Credit quality is represented by the spread between the Merrill Lynch High Yield Master Index and 30-year T-bonds.

Figure 6. Investment Style and Interest Rates, January 1980–September 1997

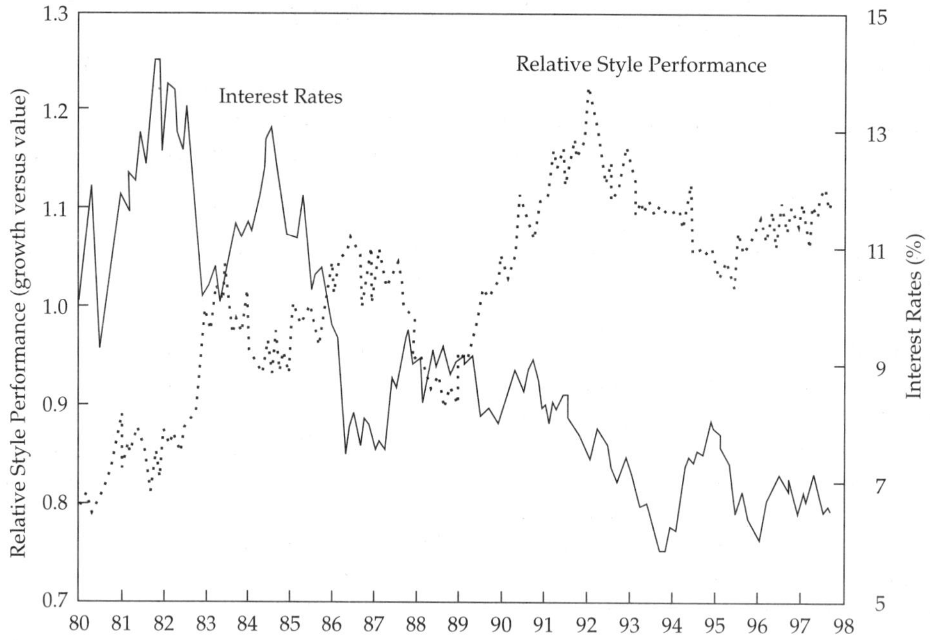

Note: Relative performance is measured by the spread between Merrill Lynch's growth and value funds. Interest rates are measured by long-term T-bonds. Correlation equals –0.8.

Figure 7. Earnings Expectations Life Cycle

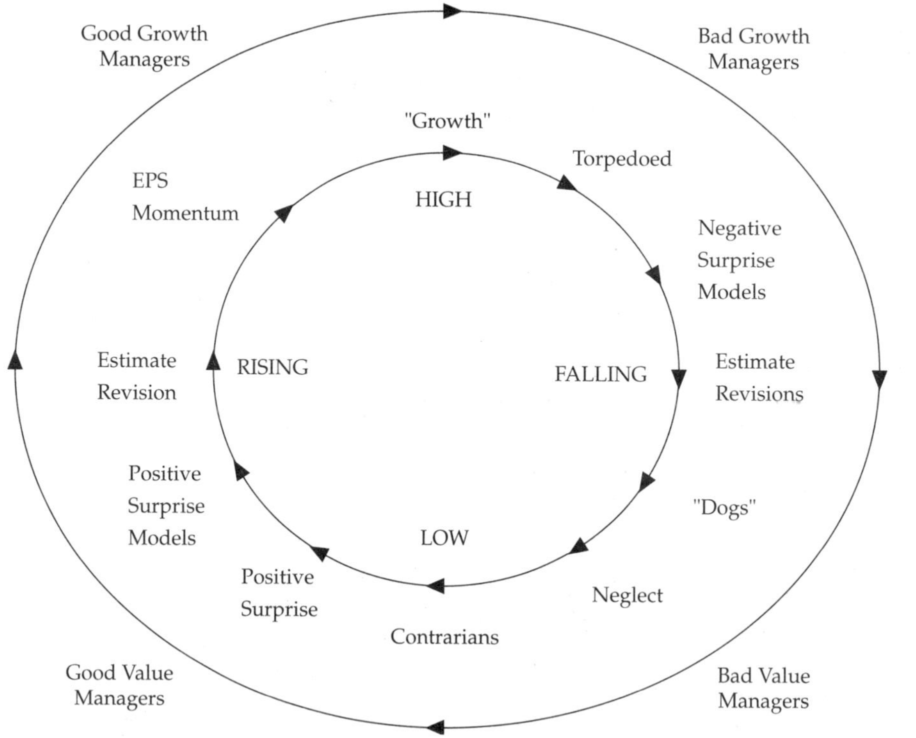

a schematic of the earnings expectations life cycle. Some companies go around the circle very quickly; some go very slowly. Individual companies may not pass through every point of the cycle; some companies may experience minicycles and repeat portions of the larger cycle as they complete the life cycle. The cycle is not perfect, but it tends to work all over the world.

Figure 7 also shows that good managers are on the left side of the circle and bad managers are on the right. Value managers are on the bottom; growth managers are on the top. Combining the two, good growth managers are in the top left quadrant and good value managers are in the bottom left quadrant.[2]

This framework yields several interesting points. First, what separates the good from the bad growth stock managers is not the stocks they are buying—which is what everybody thinks—but rather the stocks they are selling. Most people think of the contrarian as being a value manager; Figure 7 shows that a good growth stock manager also has to be a contrarian—but on the sell discipline rather than the buy discipline. Most growth managers would agree that finding a good growth stock is easier than determining when the "story is going to blow up."

Another interesting point is that value managers are hurt most by buying too early. Many value managers claim that, although they may buy early, at least they will be in the stock at the bottom. I am not sure investors should pay somebody 100 or 150 basis points (bps) to buy early. The opportunity costs of buying early can be very big. Ironically, most value managers are worried about holding stocks that are overvalued (top left quadrant of Figure 7). Although holding a stock too long may upset a consultant, it will not hurt the performance of a value manager as much as buying too early.

Thus, the key to successful investing is contrarian investing. We believe that the best strategy is to buy around "7 o'clock" on Figure 7—before positive earnings surprises—and to sell around "11 o'clock" on Figure 7—before earnings and growth momentum gets torpedoed. Thus, our model uses a mixture of value and growth measures.

Given the cycles, the obvious question is whether one can improve performance by timing styles. Our research shows that it is not possible to time styles on a tactical basis but that it is possible to time styles on a strategic basis. The most efficient frontier results from a model that combines 75 percent growth with 25 percent value investing. Perfect information will obviously outperform this static model, but being early or late by one month unfortunately results in underperformance of the static model. If investors are going to time style tactically, not only do they have to pick the correct asset, but they also have to get the timing down. Both the asset selection and the timing have to be correct, which is one of the reasons our group is not a very big fan of tactical asset allocation—too many decisions have to be made, and too many errors can result. Strategically, however, one could make changes every four or five years—and even be off by one month—and still add value.

[2]Richard Bernstein, "The Earnings Expectations Life Cycle," *Financial Analysts Journal* (March/April 1993):90–93.

Style Investing: Asia Pacific ex-Japan

The Asia Pacific ex-Japan region provides a good example of how a preferred style of investing varies by the country under consideration. Growth and value strategies work in Asia, but the success of these strategies depends on the market. Four specific countries—Australia, Hong Kong, Malaysia, and Singapore—illustrate how style rotation and profit cycles work in these various markets. Each market will be discussed in terms of the following:

- *style rotation and the profit cycle*, as related to the Asia Pacific region;
- *value strategies*, including high EPS yield (i.e., low P/E), high dividend yield, and low price-to-book (P/B), low price-to-cash earnings (P/C), and low price-to-sales (P/S) ratios;
- *growth strategies*, including trailing, or reported, EPS momentum, forward or forecasted EPS momentum, and a simple estimate revision model—whether brokers are issuing upgrades or downgrades;
- *predictiveness of brokers' optimism*, which is a strategy based on broker buy/sell decisions; and
- *earnings momentum, value, and optimism*, which is a strategy based on all three styles.

Australia

In Australia, the profit cycle seems to have picked up in 1997; if true, value strategies should be expected to continue to outperform. The best performing value strategies appear to be low P/E, low P/B, and low P/C. Broker optimism alone does not have much predictive power, but combining earnings momentum, value, and brokers' optimism is an extremely good way of picking stocks. In terms of the earnings expectation life cycle, the best strategy is to select stocks around 6 or 7 o'clock, as shown in Figure 7, when expectations are high but the stocks are still cheap.

Cycles of Style Rotation and the Profit Cycle. Australia has four distinct periods of style rotation and profit cycles, as **Figure 8** shows. At Merrill Lynch, we have found that the absolute level of EPS growth is not important; what is important is the way expectations move. From January 1989 through mid-1991, EPS growth and expectations fell. In the following four years, growth became more excessive, and EPS growth forecasts rose. Then Australia saw a 12-month period in which the growth forecast fell off quite dramatically, and in the first three quarters of 1997, bottom-up EPS growth forecasts in Australia generally started to improve.

Figure 8. Australia: Growth versus Value Relative Performance and EPS Growth Forecasts, January 1989–August 1997

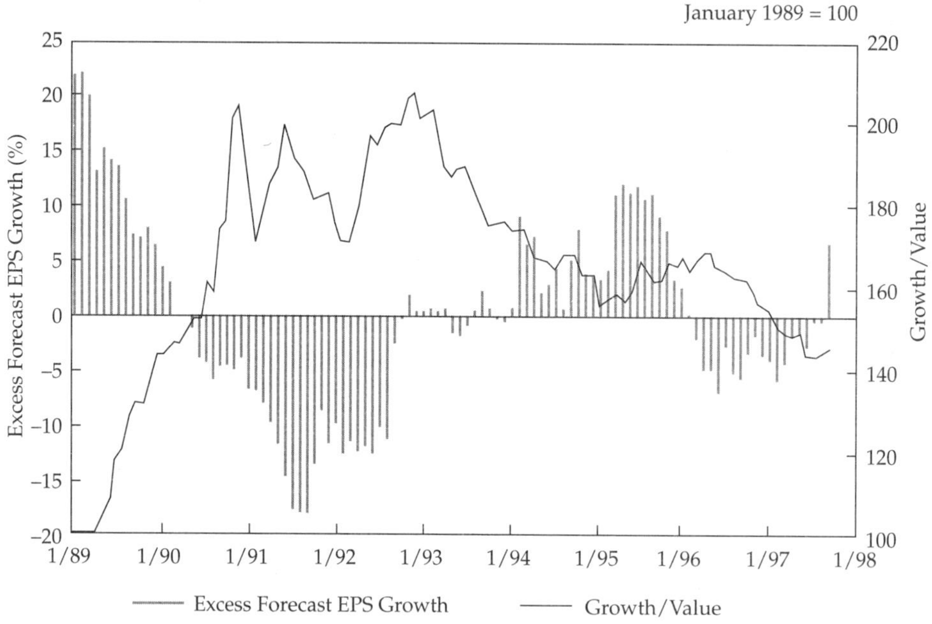

Note: Excess forecast EPS growth is calculated as the market capitalization weighted average percentage change in EPS from reported (t) to forecast ($t + 1$) less the long-term average.

Source: Based on data from I/B/E/S International and MSCI.

We make a generalization as to whether growth strategies outperform value strategies. We simply take an average of the performance of the growth strategies and look at their performance relative to the value strategies. When the line in Figure 8 is rising (upward sloping), growth strategies have been outperforming value strategies. When the line is falling (downward sloping), value strategies have been outperforming growth strategies.

By looking at the relationship between the profit cycle and relative performance of styles from January 1989 through mid-1991, we can see that when the profit cycle decelerated, profits become more scarce, and growth strategies outperformed. From mid-1991 through 1996, as the profit cycle picked up, growth generally became more abundant. How do investors pick among all of those stocks that are growing? They pick the cheap stocks, thus becoming value investors, and value strategies outperform growth strategies. For the first three quarters in 1997, the profit cycle in Australia has been improving. Growth is abundant, and therefore, value strategies have been outperforming and should continue to outperform, which explains why many of the new fund managers in Australia are value managers.

Value Strategies. The relative performance of the three best performing value strategies in Australia—high EPS yield (i.e., low P/E), low P/B, and low P/C—is shown in **Figure 9**. The profile of these three styles is very similar through time. These styles underperformed from December 1988 to December 1990, and since then, they have generally outperformed because of what has happened to profits in Australia. For the 1988–90 period, not only did growth strategies outperform value strategies, as the rising line in Figure 8 demonstrates, but value strategies also generally underperformed, as the falling line in Figure 9 indicates. Interestingly, one of the most successful value strategies in Australia during the 1990–97 period has been low P/E. The P/B strategy and P/C strategy were also successful in Australia during this time period.

Growth Strategies. Although value strategies are currently successful in Australia, one growth strategy—investing in stocks with recent upward earnings revisions—has consistently worked well, as shown in **Figure 10**. This growth strategy simply looks at the percentage of brokers upgrading earnings revisions from the prior month.

Brokers' Optimism. When it comes to brokers' optimism, the good news is that over the 1993–97 period, the bulls outperformed the bears. The performance through time is not consistent, however, and in Australia, brokers' recommendations do not appear to hold incredible amounts of predictive power. **Figure 11** shows brokers' buy/sell recommendations. In general, from mid-1993 to mid-1996, brokers' buy

Figure 9. Australia: Comparison of Value Strategies, December 1988–September 1997

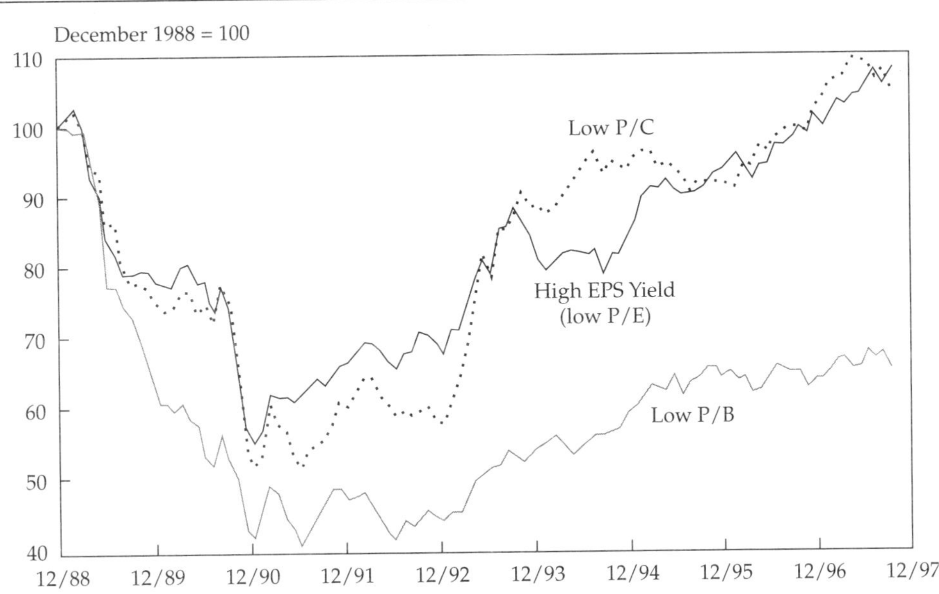

Note: Relative total return versus equal-weighted MSCI country index.

Source: Based on data from MSCI.

Figure 10. Australia: EPS Revisions, December 1988–September 1997

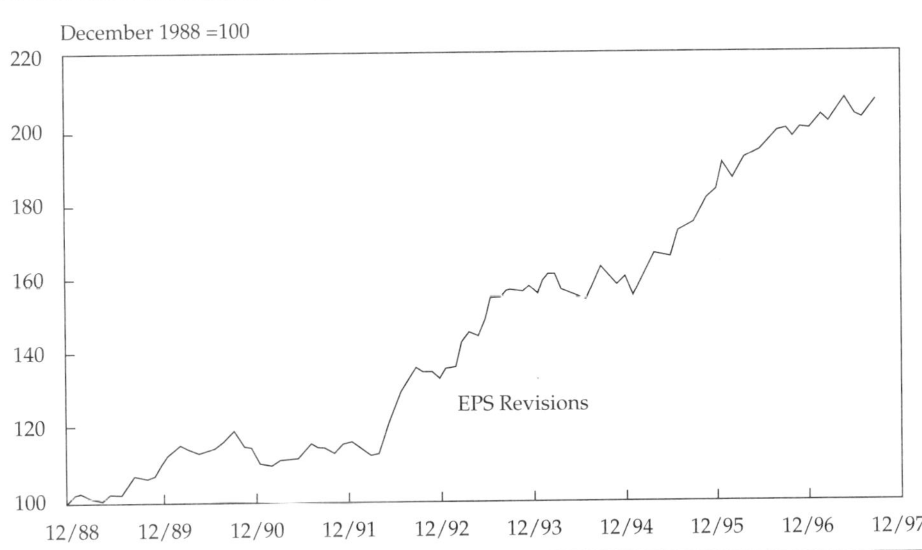

Note. Relative total return versus equal-weighted MSCI country index.

Source: Based on data from I/B/E/S International and MSCI.

recommendations outperformed, but since mid-1996, they have not. Brokers' sell recommendations have been trending down since December 1994. In other words, they have been underperforming.

Earnings Momentum, Value, and Optimism. We have started running a model that combines earnings momentum, value, and optimism. We take the best Australian growth strategy (earnings revisions), add in P/E (one of the best performing value strategies), and factor in a bit of broker optimism. We have placed the most weight on earnings revisions, the second most weight on value, and the lightest weight on optimism. Although this model has only been running since March 1997, the combination of those three factors has proven to be a very successful way of selecting attractive stocks and avoiding unattractive stocks in Australia. Since March 1997,

Figure 11. Australia: Brokers' Optimism, June 1993–September 1997

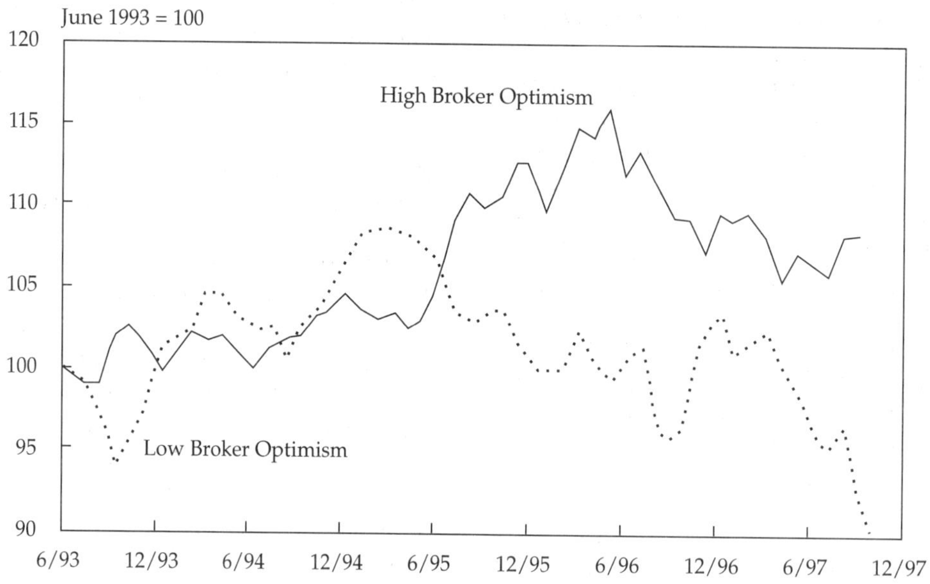

Note: Cumulative performance relative to all ordinaries.
Source: Based on data from *The Estimate Directory*.

the long portfolio has outperformed by 5.4 percent and the short portfolio, which is expected to underperform, underperformed by 23.7 percent, as shown in **Figure 12**.

Hong Kong

Because corporate profits are stalling in Hong Kong, value strategies, which have been outperforming, are expected to start underperforming. As growth becomes more scarce in Hong Kong, growth strategies are expected to pick up and start outperforming. The best value strategies have certainly been low P/E, P/C, and P/S. We have found that broker optimism has predictive value and our model that

Figure 12. Australia: Performance of Earnings Momentum, Value, and Optimism Model, March 5, 1997, to October 1, 1997

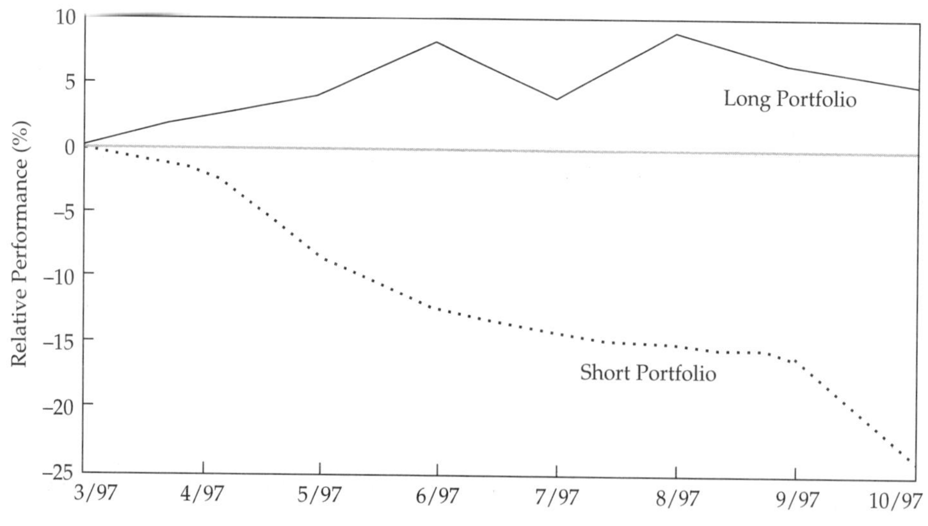

incorporates earnings momentum, value, and optimism has outperformed as expected.

Cycles of Style Rotation and the Profit Cycle. The relationship between the profit cycle and the performance of growth and value in Hong Kong is not as clear as in Australia over the long term. But in the past few years, the relationship has been very strong, as **Figure 13** shows. From January 1994 to January 1996, profits were becoming scarce. What did investors do? They bid up the price of the stocks that maintained growth, so growth strategies outperformed value. Therefore, as growth has become more abundant, value strategies have been outperforming growth strategies. In the 1996–97 period, growth forecasts have actually been picking up in Hong Kong, although the effect of the Asian currency crisis will probably dampen EPS growth. The consensus seems to be that the profit cycle will slow down in Hong Kong as a result of the currency crisis. Therefore, investors would be better off concentrating on growth strategies in Hong Kong because in a period when EPS declines, growth strategies tend to outperform.

Value Strategies. Value strategies have worked extremely well in Hong Kong during the December 1988 to third quarter 1997 period. Relative total returns using the low P/E and low price-to-trailing-EPS strategies have outperformed an equal-weighted MSCI country index. Recently in Hong Kong, the star performer has been low P/C. In fact, P/C and P/S regionally have recently been very successful strategies in picking stocks that are expected to outperform. These strategies do not always work over time, but if investors can determine in general when growth will outperform value, then they will have an opportunity to pick which stocks will outperform.

Growth Strategies. The reported EPS growth strategy (selecting stocks that reported the biggest growth rate last year) is the most successful growth strategy in Hong Kong, as **Figure 14** shows. Nevertheless, periods exist when forecasted EPS growth dramatically outperforms, and similarly with earnings revisions through time. Over the past couple of years, earnings revisions have also outperformed; relative total returns have increased 15 percent between 1995 and 1997.

Brokers' Optimism. Brokers' buy/sell recommendations in Hong Kong have worked exceptionally well. Cumulative returns for broker buy recommendations relative to the Hang Seng Index have outperformed from mid-1993 through mid-1997. If investors simply listened to their brokers

Figure 13. Hong Kong: Growth versus Value Relative Performance and EPS Growth Forecasts, January 1989–August 1997

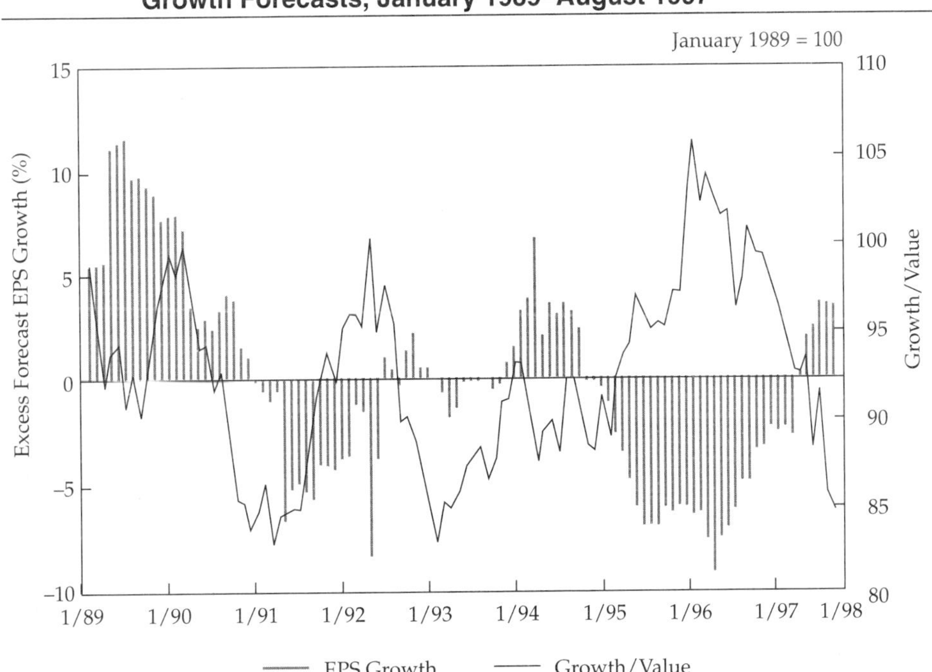

Note: Excess forecast EPS growth is calculated as the market capitalization weighted average percentage change in EPS from reported (t) to forecast (t +1) less the long-term average.

Source: Based on data from I/B/E/S International and MSCI.

Figure 14. Hong Kong: Growth Strategies, December 1988–September 1997

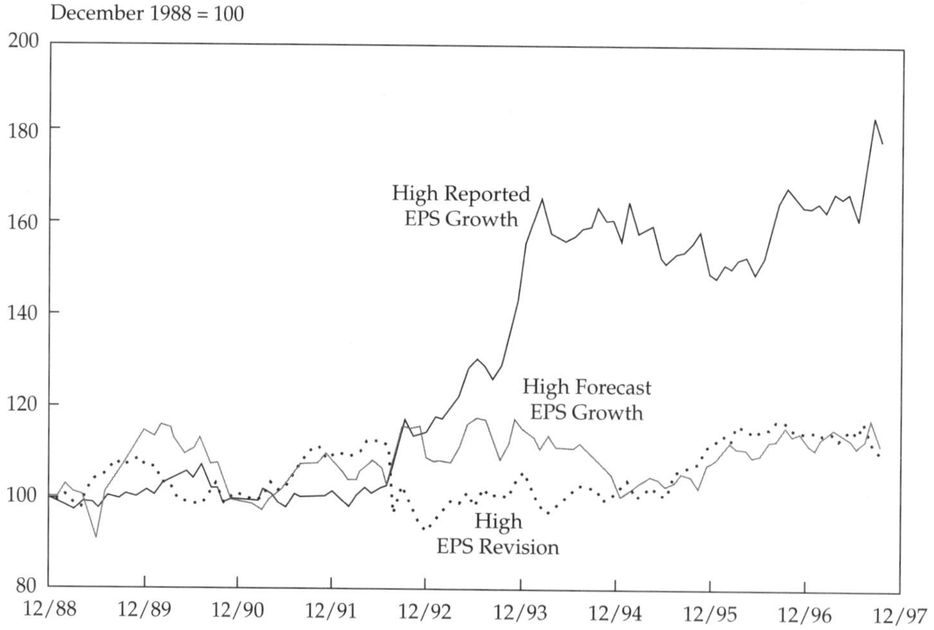

Note: Relative total return versus equal-weighted MSCI country index.

Source: Based on data from I/B/E/S International and MSCI.

when they called up and said, "Buy this stock," typically, investors would have done well. Similarly, if investors listened to their brokers when they said, "Sell this stock," typically, they would actually have added performance. If they had held the stock, they would have underperformed; cumulative total performance declined by about 40 percent during the same period. So, our analysis suggests that during the past four or so years in Hong Kong, broker optimism has been very effective as a style in picking stocks that will outperform and underperform.

Earnings Momentum, Value, and Optimism. The model that combines value, growth, and optimism in Hong Kong has been running for more than two years. This model shows that the long portfolio has outperformed by 47 percent; the short portfolio has underperformed by almost 54 percent, as shown in **Figure 15**. The consistency of that performance is quite staggering. Note the amount of predictive information gained from looking at earnings revisions, at simple P/Es, and at a model that selects purchasing stocks just before positive earnings sur-

Figure 15. Hong Kong: Performance of Earnings Momentum, Value, and Optimism Model, September 18, 1995–September 1997

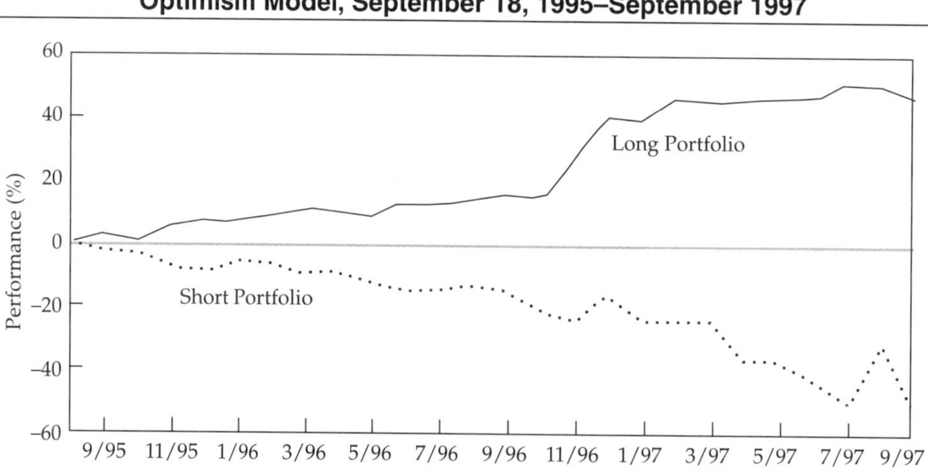

Note: Relative performance of buy and sell models.

prises and selling stocks when earnings expectations are declining and the stocks are expensive.

Malaysia

Because the profit cycle is faltering in Malaysia, value strategies, which have been working, are expected to start underperforming and growth strategies are expected to start outperforming. The best performing value strategies have been low P/E, P/B, and P/S, but earnings revision models are likely to become a very successful way of picking stocks in the future. Broker optimism is not consistently predictive in Malaysia, and on the sell side, it definitely adds no value. The model of earnings momentum, value, and optimism has added some value through time.

Cycles of Style Rotation and the Profit Cycle. Malaysia is an interesting case. The profit forecasts and the EPS growth forecasts have been quite stable, although only four years of data are available. The deviation from average growth rates has not changed much. The relative performance of value versus growth is declining, which indicates that value strategies have been successful in Malaysia during the past four years. In late 1997, however, Malaysia has been at a turning point. EPS forecasts have fallen off dramatically, in terms of bottom-up market EPS growth forecasts. If general consensus is true, then EPS growth will continue to slide, and for the first time in our analysis of Malaysia, we believe growth strategies will start to outperform value strategies. The stocks to own in Malaysia will be the ones that can maintain their growth rates and have earnings upgrades; the strategy may be as simple as buying stocks that have reported high EPS growth rates. Given the 1997 currency crisis in Asia, maintaining high EPS growth rates will be quite challenging.

Value Strategies. Value strategies in Malaysia during the 1993–97 period have been the star performers. Relative total returns for value strategies have far exceeded an equal-weighted MSCI country index. Once again, low P/E is a star performer, as are P/B and P/S.

Growth Strategies. Among growth strategies in Malaysia, the earnings revisions strategy has been the best performer, although in 1997, it has not added that much value. The underperformance of stocks that have high forecasted EPS growth is surprising to most people. The most commonly used investment style in Asia, and probably globally, is picking stocks that are forecasted to have the biggest growth rate, but an investment strategy based on forecasted EPS growth has been a consistent underperformer in Malaysia. Malaysia, however, is at a turning point. If EPS growth falls off substantially, then these growth strategies should become successful.

Brokers' Optimism. In Malaysia, unlike Hong Kong, brokers' recommendations do not appear to hold much predictive power. In fact, in the chaos of 1997, brokers' buy recommendations have not only underperformed but also lost any value added over the 1996–97 period, as shown in **Figure 16**. Similarly, brokers' sell recommendations have not added to performance at all.

Earnings Momentum, Value, and Optimism. The model that combines earnings momentum, value, and optimism in Malaysia has been running

Figure 16. Malaysia: Brokers' Optimism, June 1993–September 1997

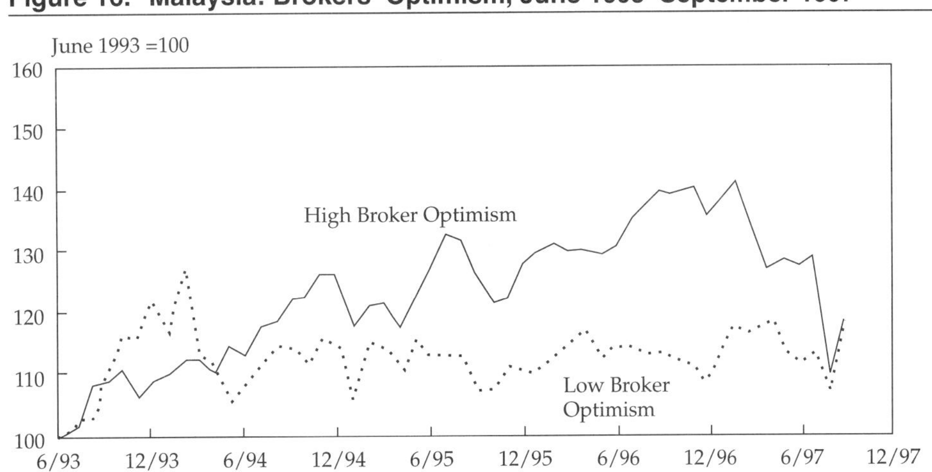

Note: Cumulative performance relative to the Kuala Lumpur Composite Index.

Source: Based on data from *The Estimate Directory*.

only since March 1996. Since inception, the long portfolio and the short portfolio have added little performance, although for the first 18 months after inception, the performance added was quite stellar.

Fund managers may be encouraged to learn that some quantitative techniques have worked historically in Malaysia, although they have not worked during the 1997 currency crisis. We believe quantitative models simply quantify fundamentals. Thus, as the profit cycle turns in Malaysia, we expect the earnings revisions strategy coupled with the value strategy, which has been consistently outperforming, to be one of the best ways of picking stocks. We expect this model to continue to outperform.

Singapore

Because the profit cycle is heading down in Singapore, we do not expect value to start outperforming growth. At Merrill Lynch, our top-down forecast shows that Singapore may be one of the first countries to have an improvement in the profit cycle. Until that improvement actually happens, we expect growth strategies to continue to outperform value strategies. All three growth styles that we monitor have proven to work equally well. Brokers' buy recommendations tend to add some performance in Singapore, but on the sell side, we find little predictive power.

Cycles of Style Rotation and the Profit Cycle. The profit cycle in Singapore has been falling during the 1995–97 period, which indicates that growth strategies have generally been outperforming value strategies. Nevertheless, as **Figure 17** shows, when growth forecasts did not change much during the January 1993 to January 1996 period, neither growth nor value dominated. If the profit cycle continues to decline, as most investors believe, then our theory suggests growth strategies will continue to outperform in Singapore.

P/B and P/S have been the best value strategies in Singapore. Certainly, P/B has been a consistent outperformer through time, but during the 1996–97 period, P/S has been a star performer.

The three growth strategies that we monitor (EPS growth, forecasted EPS growth, and earnings revisions) have been outperforming dramatically during the 1994–97 period. We expect these strategies to continue to outperform.

Brokers' Optimism. Although brokers' buy recommendations tend to predict the outperformance of stocks relative to the Strait Times Index in Singapore, they have lost a bit of that performance in the second half of 1997. In general, the buys outperform the sells, but the predictive power of brokers' recommendations in Singapore is limited as an investment style.

Earnings Momentum, Value, and Optimism. Combining the three factors—earnings momentum, value, and optimism—in Singapore added only a few percentage points over and above the Strait Times Index during 1997. This model has worked extremely well at times, but since the fall of 1997, it has been unsuccessful. Nevertheless, we expect growth strategies to continue to outperform in Singapore and earnings revisions to be one of the best ways of picking stocks as the profit cycle continues to decelerate.

Asia Pacific Conclusions

In Australia, we suggest that investors overweight value strategies. We expect the value strategies that have been working recently to continue to work as the profit cycle continues to pick up. In Hong Kong, as late as September 1997, the profit cycle was continuing to pick up, but the profit cycle seems to have changed direction. In light of the Asian currency crisis, the profit cycle will probably start to decelerate in Hong Kong, in which case, growth may well start to outperform in Hong Kong. In Malaysia, the situation is similar. Because the profit cycle is starting to fall, we expect growth to start outperforming value. Growth has been working in Singapore as an investment style, and we expect it to continue to outperform value and the normal market indexes as the profit cycle continues to be weak.

Implications of Style Investing

All equity markets, without exception, are segmented. In fact, even within the United States, the market can be subdivided, and segments can still be found within the subdivisions. Within an industry, for example, both high-quality and low-quality stocks exist. Markets are segmented because of structural, psychological, and informational factors. Again, the structural factors are the investment-charter-type issues. Psychological factors are regret aversion versus risk aversion and those types of factors. Informational factors include information asymmetry.

Investors need to pay attention to style rotation even if they are disciplined investors. Again, remember the example of low P/E investing in the United States. This strategy has certainly worked over the long term, but exceptions in the short term do exist, for example, around 1990, when a lot of value managers went out of business.

Figure 17. Singapore: Growth versus Value Relative Performance and EPS Growth Forecasts, January 1989–September 1997

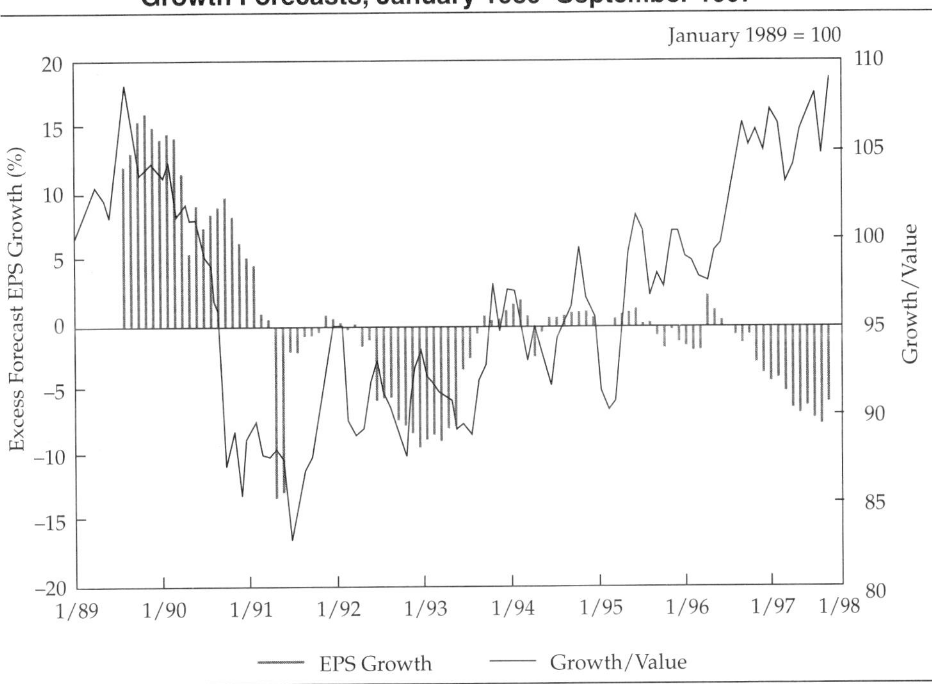

Note: Excess forecast EPS growth is calculated as the market capitalization weighted average percentage change in EPS from reported (t) to forecast (t +1) less the long-term average.

Source: Based on data from I/B/E/S International and MSCI .

Many microeconomic and macroeconomic factors influence and help predict style rotation, but by far the most important is the profit cycle. Expectations also play a major role in style rotation. Investors can easily say that managers should be buying good companies (or not) at different points in time, but the question is how people define a "good company." Will they all have the same expectations about what is a good company? Probably not.

Finally, we think strategic allocation can add value, but tactical allocation, with its reliance on correct timing and asset selection, is a waste of time.

Question and Answer Session

Richard Bernstein
Nigel Tupper

Question: What is your view of small-cap investing as a style itself?

Bernstein: I think it is a very good strategy over the long term. People often think of small-cap stocks in the United States as being emerging growth stocks; in fact, long-term performance statistics show that the small-cap stocks that outperform in the United States happen to be small-cap value stocks. The index that goes back to 1926 in the United States has nothing to do with emerging growth investing; it is all down-and-out companies that used to be big. Thus, over the long term, small-cap value works exceptionally well.

Small-cap value is not tremendously different from our index of C and D rated stocks. The same themes apply to both, which explains why our C and D index performs so well through time. The C and D index compounds annually at about 19 percent a year in the United States. For the same time period, the S&P 500 was about 13 percent a year, so our index shows substantial outperformance. Even if you take into account transaction costs, our index will not eat up 600 bps of outperformance. Small-cap investing is an important theme and a good investment style.

The question with small-cap stocks is always, "Are they investable?" A couple of years ago, Bill Fouse had an article in the *Financial Analysts Journal* that argued that the small-cap effect was all a myth because investors could not invest in small-cap stocks.[1] The article, however, did not address the fact that cycles affect the performance of small-cap stocks. Why are there certain points in time when small-cap stocks outperform, and why are there points in time when they underperform? Does small-cap investing work on the margin? The important points to remember are that cycles exist and style rotation works for *smaller* stocks. You do not just have to look at small stocks.

Question: Given the relatively narrow universe of stocks analyzed in Asia, how valid is your assessment of value investing, which in Asia typically has a small-cap bias?

Tupper: The assumption is that value strategies do not have small-cap biases. Our analysis certainly has some bias, because we have taken out those smaller stocks, but we still show that the profit cycle can be used to predict when growth styles will outperform value styles, and vice versa. A more detailed analysis of the market-cap distribution within each of those styles would provide further insight.

Bernstein: No matter where you are—the United States, Europe, or elsewhere—value strategies generally will use small-cap companies and growth strategies will tend to use large-cap companies. What is important from our perspective is the focus on the profit cycle as an indicator of which style to use, and that focus does not vary by country.

Question: Please comment on the effectiveness of risk measured by either beta or standard deviation of the stocks involved in your various strategies versus the risk of the benchmark index used.

Tupper: Most of the investment styles that we studied have a higher standard deviation of return than the market indexes. In Asia Pacific, it is quite difficult to get investment styles with a low standard deviation of return as a measure of risk. In terms of beta, our analysis suggests that the theory that high beta stocks outperform when markets are going up, and vice versa, does not hold true; the relationship does not appear to be strong. So, the predictive power of beta within Asia Pacific is quite limited.

Question: Is it too early to say that C and D rated stocks outperform A rated stocks in the long term?

Bernstein: Yes, it probably is too early. In 1991, our C and D index was up 90 percent. The index absolutely exploded when the market began to realize that the economy was coming out of the recession.

The best way to analyze this question is to review some of the junk bond studies. Remember, the quality considerations in the stock market and in the bond market were very tight during the past 11 years. Junk bond studies certainly show that the junk bonds performed well. In fact, they were not called junk bonds in those studies; "junk bonds" is a term of the 1980s, and these studies were done before then. In these studies, they were just called non-investment-grade bonds. These studies basically used the same argument that Michael Milken used to show that

[1]William L. Fouse, "The Small Stocks Hoax," *Financial Analysts Journal* (July/August 1989):12–15.

non-investment-grade bonds performed very, very well. Investors get capital appreciation as the bond's credit rating moves up, which is exactly what happens on the stock side as a company goes from being a C to a B to an A rated stock—more and more people begin to invest. As the rating improves, performance goes up, and investors receive very high income at the beginning of this process.

Question: What is the average market cap of the C and D stocks in your study? Are they investable for large institutional investors?

Bernstein: The C and D stocks tend to be smaller companies. The average market cap of an A+ stock in mid-October 1997 was about US$15 billion. The average market cap of a C or D stock was about US$1 billion. Although they tend to be small, the Cs and Ds are investable. A lot of stocks are in that universe that people invest in regularly, for instance, airlines.

Even if you think C and D rated stocks are not investable, remember that a lot of the analysis I showed works on the margin. So, maybe you are not going to buy the *lowest* quality stocks, but the effect will work if you buy *lower* quality stocks. Our B– index, which I did not show, has been performing quite well in the past several months, as have the Cs and Ds. The B– stocks are also undoubtedly a very investable universe.

Question: Do you have model results with forward earnings growth?

Tupper: In our analysis, we looked at creating three market forecast EPS growth rates for each of the markets within Asia Pacific. First, we used reported EPS growth. Second, we used the next fiscal year's EPS forecast divided by the prior year's EPS forecast, which is a short-term forecast, and third, we created a 12-month rolling forward EPS forecast, bottom-up. In our analysis, we found that the second method was the most predictive of investment style performance within the Asia Pacific region. If you use reported EPS growth, the relationship between investment styles and the profit cycle still exists, although there is a lag. The 12-month rolling forward market EPS forecast was not as predictive as simply looking at a shorter period, for example, FY_1 EPS over FY_0 EPS.

Bernstein: One member in our group, Markus Barth, has looked at 10 to 20 European markets to see whether trailing earnings momentum or forward earnings momentum is a better predictor of stock prices. He found that cycles exist, and depending on where the market is in the profit cycle, sometimes the market becomes very forward looking and sometimes it becomes very backward looking. Obviously, the more aggressive the growth forecast as the profit cycle begins to accelerate, the more people look forward; as it begins to decelerate, they look backward.

Question: Is it true that when EPS growth is abundant, value strategies will outperform growth strategies? If so, why have growth investors done better than value investors during the past few years in the United States, when EPS growth has been quite strong?

Bernstein: It is not the growth rate itself that matters but the change in the growth rate. For example, if you look at the profit cycle in the United States that was shown in Figure 3, you will notice the cycle actually peaked in the first quarter of 1995. Earnings growth for the S&P 500 at that time was 45 percent, but that growth slowed to only 1 percent in mid-1996. During that period when earnings growth slowed from 45 percent to 1 percent, growth styles substantially outperformed value. When the earnings growth rate went from 1 percent to 18 percent, value investors did a little better than growth investors. Currently, the profit cycle in the United States has begun to roll over—going from 18 percent to 14 percent—and growth has again begun to outperform.

So, you cannot simply say a market will experience EPS growth of 12 percent and use that number to make a value/growth decision; you have to compare current EPS growth with the long-term average. If EPS growth was 5 percent and now you expect 12 percent growth, then you want to be a value investor. If EPS growth is expected to grow at 12 percent and it was growing at 15 percent, then you want to be a growth investor. It is the acceleration or deceleration of profit growth that drives these cycles.

Question: Please define excess forecast EPS growth.

Tupper: Excess forecast EPS growth is calculated as the market capitalization weighted average percentage change in EPS from reported (t) to forecast (t +1) less the long-term average. This factor indicates when growth is excessive or when it is at subnormal levels.

Question: What universe of stocks do you use for the Hong Kong and Singapore averages? Do you only use those in the MSCI index or a wider selection?

Tupper: In most of our analyses, we typically try to create a universe of stocks that is available to institutional investors. In our earnings momentum, value, and optimism analysis, we use a universe in Hong Kong of about 95 stocks.

They represent stocks with a market cap greater than US$500 million, a turnover rate greater than half a million a day on average over the previous six months, and coverage by at least five brokers. Using the same constraints in Singapore, we came up with a universe of about 41 stocks. In Malaysia and Australia, these constraints produced a universe of about 94 stocks in each market.

Question: Did you account for foreign premiums and investability when back testing your model?

Tupper: Yes to both. Where foreign premium stocks exist, we have used these stocks within the analysis. We perform a three-stage filter in terms of investability within our earnings momentum, value, and optimism analysis in the Asia Pacific region. First, we filter out anything that is too small in terms of size. Second, we filter out anything that has low turnover. Third, we filter out anything that is not covered by a reasonable number of brokers. All of the stocks within the analysis are typically large, well-covered stocks that have enough turnover for institutional investors to analyze. We have introduced some bias into some of the analysis, but in doing so, we make it practical for institutional investors.

Question: Do you think that the quality of the research affects the performance of the Kuala Lumpur market?

Tupper: Predicting which investment styles will outperform in Kuala Lumpur is difficult at times. In certain markets, people often think that some factors other than fundamentals drive the markets. Investors often talk about political risk or the lack of quality research and mention Kuala Lumpur at the same time. Those nonfundamental factors can have a big influence on the Kuala Lumpur market and on the Malaysian market, but these markets are not completely unpredictable. For example, from April 1996 to October 1997, earnings revisions and low P/E have been very successful styles to use in Malaysia. We believe that some styles do work very well in Malaysia and that we can still use the profit cycle to predict which styles in general will outperform or underperform.

Question: What would you expect of Thailand?

Tupper: Our analysis of Thailand showed that earnings revisions were not predictive, that broker optimism was not predictive, and that P/E analysis was not predictive. I have heard of studies showing that trailing P/Es are predictive in Thailand, but all of our analysis has shown very little predictive power in most investment styles in Thailand, which is one of the reasons we do not concentrate on it as much as other countries. A lot of fund managers have said to me recently that they think investment styles will work in Thailand from now on. We will continue to monitor investment styles in Thailand to see if they start to work.

Style Analysis in Major Non-U.S. Markets

Robert J. Schwob
Chief Executive
Style Investment Research Associates Limited

In international equity markets, style analysis is a relevant and important portfolio management tool. International markets are different from and more complex than the U.S. equity market, so styles must be applied carefully with regard to local market characteristics. Styles are important on their own, but sector influences can often hide trends or mislead managers. Thus, sector-adjusted data can help managers distinguish style tilts from sector decisions.

Style analysis involves many aspects of fund management and is perhaps one of the most important innovations in equity analysis. At its core, style analysis is nothing more than a rational reduction of the immense data set of about 25,000 companies listed in about 30 tradable markets.

Exploring where this simple idea might lead can be fascinating. The results often make one consider what investment techniques, management practices, and investment services can be constructed based on the concept of style investing, but great care must be taken to be sure that the research is done properly. Properly defined "bottom-up" style analysis can frequently reveal much more than whether a manager is simply a value or growth manager or a large-capitalization or small-cap manager.

This presentation covers what style is, how the concept of style is currently applied, and some of the problems involved with applying style. It also deals with some of the genuine problems—the complexities, differences, and reservations—of using a style approach and shows a bit about what working within the style framework is like. The presentation ends by illustrating a way to review portfolios according to the style paradigm.

Style Analysis

Style is a way of categorizing an investment strategy. The usual style paradigm divides stocks into one of six broad categories: either value or growth and large-, mid-, or small-cap. So, a style might be large-cap value or small-cap growth. This view may be a bit simplistic and probably does not reflect the way managers actually manage, but the value versus growth and large-cap versus small-cap distinctions do have some merit. In order to search and classify stocks more accurately or with greater sensitivity, analysts look at various criteria—book-to-price ratio (B/P), dividend yield, earnings yield, cash flow yield, sales-to-price ratio (S/P), and return on equity (ROE).

Before committing to an investment style, investors must know whether the style works in the country in which they wish to invest. To assess whether styles work in specific countries, at Style Investment Research Associates we follow a formal verification procedure. First, we define a style-factor portfolio based on the stocks in that country. The portfolio is created based on a ranking of individual stocks according to specific factors. When assessing the style factors, we construct and rebalance market capitalization weighted portfolios using five steps to make sure that our selection of securities is unbiased:

- We use only information available at the time the decision would have been made.
- We include nontrading securities to avoid survivorship bias (i.e., securities that could have been purchased but have since gone out of business).
- We include income.
- We have realistic bimonthly rebalance points.
- We assess the relevance of the factor (i.e., show that the criteria actually have some foundation in economic theory or in rational finance theory).

To statistically assess the relevance of the factors, we use a Monte Carlo technique that compares the differences between the portfolios we constructed using the factor under consideration and portfolios of randomly generated stocks.[1] We assess the relevance of each style according to these conditions:

- *Identity*: The performance of stocks within each style must cluster in distinct groupings.
- *Consistency*: Securities' membership in style categories should be relatively stable.
- *Attribution*: The performance of a typical institutional portfolio should be broadly attributable to its style tilts.
- *Regularity*: The relative performance of style categories should be regular and nonrandom.
- *Universality*: All stocks should be classified using the style criteria.
- *Simplicity*: Only a limited number of clearly understandable styles should apply.

We apply formal definitions and verification processes for each category except for universality and simplicity, which are less formal. We merely identify the existence or nonexistence of these conditions as an implicit warning about using style when it may not be relevant.

The most important condition is that stocks must cluster in distinct performance groupings—that is, the identity condition. So, for each style factor under review, we estimate the likelihood that its factor-reward pattern is not simply a result of random portfolio construction, and we also try to show that the criterion actually has some foundation in economic theory and in rational finance theory.

The formal, statistical part of the identity assessment uses a Monte Carlo technique that compares the performance differences (tracking errors relative to the market) between the portfolios we construct using the factor under consideration against those (again the tracking errors) of a large number of portfolios of randomly selected stocks. With this technique, a score of 1 means 100 percent identity relevance—that is, high certainty that the portfolio performance cannot be accounted for by random portfolio construction.

At Style Investment Research Associates, we use four basic style categories: value, growth, size, and momentum. Each style is defined by a set of factors:

- *value*: B/P, dividend yield, earnings yield, cash flow yield, and S/P;
- *growth*: the negative of value or ROE, earnings growth, profit margin, and sales growth;
- *size*: market capitalization and beta; and
- *momentum*: historical relative return.

Using the six conditions, we test each style category to assess whether each factor is a theoretically and statistically valid descriptor of a style.

[1]For detailed descriptions of this technique or further information regarding the assessment techniques for other style conditions, contact the author directly at RobertSchwob@SIRA.Demon.Co.UK.

Style around the World

We have measured the identity relevance of principal style factors within each of 17 countries and found that the main styles are relevant, meaningful, and important in most markets. But because of the features of individual markets, styles must be applied with careful regard to local market characteristics.

U.S. Market. In the United States, all five factors defining the value category have an identity relevance of 100 percent and share a similar historical performance profile. This finding strongly suggests that these are important factors, which together describe a significant single style. If we were to conduct a performance attribution analysis on this basis, we would find that these factors explain a high percentage of the performance of typical institutional portfolios. Similarly, the rewards to the principal growth criteria are very similar to one another, and they mirror the rewards to the main value criteria. All of the factors have a relevance statistic of 100 percent. Although we may object on theoretical grounds that low B/P is indicative of growth, this association works as a good operational approximation in the U.S. market.

That result is not surprising for the United States. The value–growth dichotomy has a long history. Graham and Dodd introduced the idea of value in *Security Analysis*, which was published in 1934. The purpose behind that book was to try to inspire some confidence in the stock market. The United States had just come through a crash that lasted much longer than crashes are supposed to, and until that time, most people had thought only in terms of the speculative value of securities. Graham and Dodd's approach was to look at what a security is worth in terms of how much capital it had raised, how much profit it had reinvested (i.e., book value, which is shareholders' equity), and how much the company was prepared to pay shareholders—the dividend yield, another popular measure of value.

Five years after the publication of *Security Analysis*, T. Rowe Price, in a series of articles published in *Barron's*, introduced the idea of growth. He said value stocks have to bribe investors to hold them by paying high dividends (or investors drive the price to the point that the dividend and book value are attractive). Usually, these companies are already beyond their best, and they are probably on the way out. They are, as the articles described them, "mature" or "decadent" companies, which were the words used in the late 1930s to describe value companies. Price claimed that what investors really want are growth stocks: Investors could only hope to outpace inflation with growth stocks. This debate started the polarization of the U.S. investment market, which started gradually defining companies (and then managers and investment funds) as value or growth.

The value–growth polarization has not, however, occurred in other markets because they do not have the same value–growth history that the U.S. market has. Analysts need to determine what style is in non-U.S. markets, rather than simply use the value–growth labels.

Non-U.S. Markets. The value criteria are important in virtually every one of the 17 markets we study. Each of the five value factors has an identity relevance of 100 percent or near 100 percent in the four key markets of Japan, the United Kingdom, Germany, and France. The smallest figure for relevance among these markets is 70 percent in the United Kingdom for earnings yield.

Although the value factors are important, they are not synchronized or consistent from one country to another or within countries. The situation is not as straightforward as in the United States. In France, for example, whether someone wants to be a value investor depends on which factors that person uses. The indications vary, for example, when the B/P and dividend yield factors are used.

In the U.S. market, investors can look at value as the negative of growth. The return to B/P, which is the premiere value characteristic in the United States, is almost a perfect mirror image of each one of the returns to growth. Operationally, the two are the same. The paradigm of value as the negative of growth does not hold well in non-U.S. markets. Growth is important, but growth has a different definition in many of these countries. Japan, which has had a positive reward to value historically, shows no return to growth whatsoever, either positive or negative. In the United Kingdom, some evidence indicates a value–growth mirror, but it does not go across all the criteria, especially the most important criterion, sales growth. In Germany, some evidence indicates a growth–value relationship, but some of the more telling criteria of growth, such as profit margin, seem to be more like value criteria. France shows some evidence of a value–growth relationship, but the evidence is scattered as well. The identity relevance of each one of these growth factors stands by itself and could not have been accounted for simply by chance. They are individually important and must be taken into account as relevant style factors operating within each market.

Sector Sensitivity Adjustment

An obvious question arising from this analysis is whether style is simply a disguise for other industrial effects, such as those resulting from pronounced industrial cycles, interest rate movements, or exchange rate movements that affect specific sectors. There are some factual reasons why investors can live with styles being influenced by exchange rates, interest rates, or other developments within the economic cycle, but they cannot live with styles being influenced by sectors. If style-reward patterns are simply disguised industrial sector performance patterns, then investors would be better off directly examining these industrial sector trends rather than style factors. Thus, the next step in the analysis is to adjust for sectors. If sector adjustments do not have any influence, then styles have an identity of their own.

Sector adjustment goes a step further and neutralizes the effects of sector imbalances on style analysis. To analyze for sensitivity to sector movements, each company is allocated to a sector, and factor portfolios are sorted and selected sector by sector. This process, which effectively takes away the sector's influence on style, is illustrated in **Figure 1**. For example, in the United Kingdom, banks and financial companies have a high B/P and consumer stocks a low B/P. So, if analysts were to conduct a style analysis without adjusting for sectors, they would get a high concentration of banks and a low representation of consumer stocks in the value portfolio. Knowing that U.K. banks have a high B/P and consumer stocks have a low B/P gives the analyst additional information with which to work.

Sector adjustment makes little difference in the United States, which has been good for style and certainly obviates the need to apply sector adjustments. Barr Rosenberg's first multifactor analysis of the U.S. market adjusted for sectors through the use of dummy variables. Subsequent analyses by some of his students omitted sector adjustments and found only marginal differences in results. Similarly, early research by Jacobs and Levy in 1993 analyzed factor contributions to security returns with and without sector adjustments. Their results showed significant nonrandom influences on returns from several factors, but how one adjusts for sectors has become a bit random. So far, none of the major commercial style index providers offers sector-adjusted data.

In most cases, international style and sector adjustments do not make a difference besides minor effects on the scale and magnitude of the style effects. But in some instances—the United Kingdom for value, Germany for growth, and France for value—sector adjustments make a significant difference (i.e., turning points can be seen much more clearly with sector-adjusted data). For this reason, sector/style adjustments are very important.

Style managers should be measured against a

Figure 1. Sector Adjustment in Style Analysis

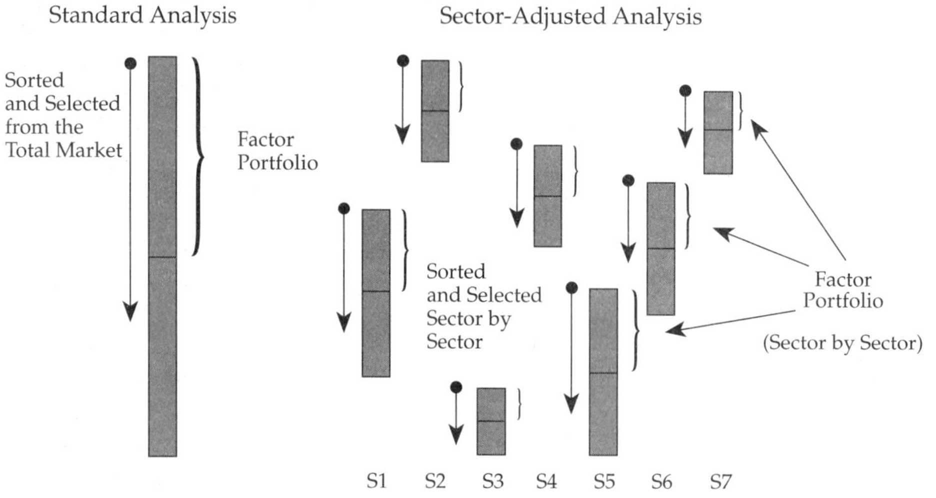

Standard Analysis | Sector-Adjusted Analysis

Sorted and Selected from the Total Market

Factor Portfolio

Sorted and Selected Sector by Sector

Factor Portfolio (Sector by Sector)

S1 S2 S3 S4 S5 S6 S7

Note: S1 = Sector 1, S2 = Sector 2, etc.

sector-adjusted benchmark, because implicit in the analysis of the standard style approach is the belief that managers will shift and alter sector exposures according to their style analysis, rather than implementing the style within the sectors. For most managers, this assumption is unrealistic. Managers generally consider sector-allocation decisions as distinct from style decisions, which supports the use of sector-adjusted benchmarks to evaluate performance.

Australia is a vivid example of a market where sector adjustment makes a big difference. One of the anomalies of the Australian market is that local banks have high dividends, high B/Ps, and somewhat curiously high ROEs. Thus, Australian banks are both value and growth companies. In Australia, both value and growth outperformed over the recent period, so the only way to disentangle the various influences on returns is to do the sector adjustment. Neutralizing the effects of large size and divergent performance of the financial sector allows the portfolio manager to focus on pure style influences.

In summary, even after sector adjustment, key style factors are relevant in the major non-U.S. markets, although identity statistics fall sharply in Australia and Singapore. In the majority of cases, style does not simply capture sector influences. The effects are not synchronized across markets or within markets. Of the 17 major markets we have looked at, each market has at least two relevant sector-adjusted value factors, and the majority of the sector-adjusted growth factors are also relevant; however, the relevant factors may differ from market to market. Size is almost always important.

Working in the Style Framework

At Style Investment Research Associates, we look at markets according to three different but related cycles: the interest rate cycle, the economic cycle, and the market cycle. **Figure 2** depicts how the market cycle tends to lead the economic cycle and the economic cycle tends to lead the interest rate cycle.

The attractiveness and relative performance of each of the styles changes throughout each cycle. For example, value stocks benefit during periods of high or volatile medium-term interest rates, although evidence suggests that rising short-term interest rates have the opposite effect. With value stocks, investors get their money up front; they are buying genuine near-term value—up-front dividends and current book value. Investors are comforted knowing they own shares in a company with a high dividend and a high book value, which is the duration argument. A high dividend and a high book value will benefit investors when interest rates are high or volatile. Conversely, investors will be less inclined to have the patience to hold growth stocks.

Because value companies tend to be small and weak, their price discount to estimated value is the inducement, or bribe, that the company offers investors to hold them. These companies do better on an economic rebound than growth companies and may do better on a market rebound because value companies have extra sensitivity to changes in business sentiment. Value companies often do better as the market is topping out and growth companies are pulling back a bit, especially those that have been overvalued. Bernstein and Tupper suggested that the value and growth cycle is really a credit and a profit

Figure 2. Value Cycle as a Function of Market, Economic, and Interest Rate Cycles

A. Market Cycle

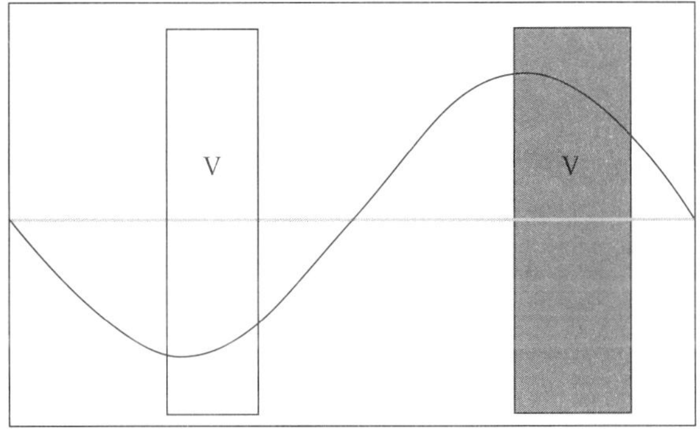

B. Economic Cycle

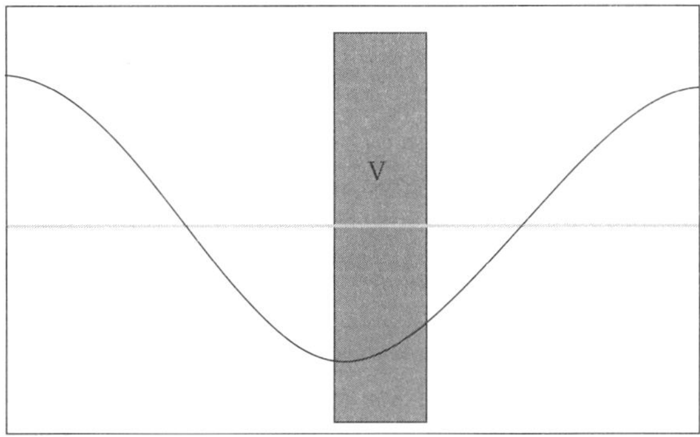

C. Interest Rate Cycle

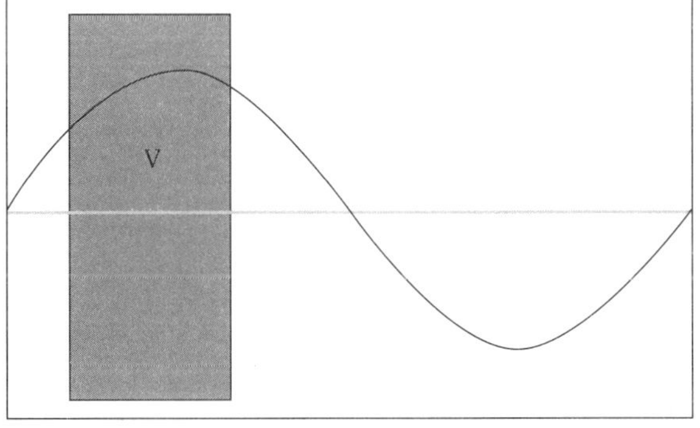

cycle, which can be seen in our work as well.[2] Profitability and profit expectations tend to increase in the trough of an economic cycle for a number of reasons, such as corporate restructuring and cost savings. Consequently, the profit outlook improves in anticipation of economic recovery. According to Bernstein and Tupper, when profits are abundant, investors search for value stocks—not profitability because it is everywhere—and, as in our view, value outperforms growth. When profits are less abundant, investors search out and bid up the prices of profitable growth companies that offer a scarce resource.

Clearly, value stocks tend to outperform at the "nervous" peak of the cycle, as recently overpromoted, larger, and more liquid growth stocks pull back. The behavior of value, however, is less clear during the early phase of a forming bull market. Although researchers frequently argue that professional investors will swoop to buy undervalued stocks as they get a glimmer of a market rise, as the market turns upward, it attracts the attention of nondomestic investors, hedge fund managers, and mutual fund managers. These investors focus on liquidity and name recognition, which are principally growth-stock characteristics.

At the moment, we forecast a modest return to value for the coming months, as shown in **Table 1**. We believe that the market cycle is being pulled wider, so the peak of the market cycle has now gone beyond the peak of the economic cycle. Consequently, I would argue that we are close to the peak of the market cycle, where we should see a changeover from a period of success for companies that have been growth oriented to a period of success for value companies. The full-fledged turn toward value will come only when the market anticipates a sharp positive turn in the economic cycle. Without the positive turn in the cycle, the rebound for value stocks will be short lived.

Case Study

A bottom-up style analysis provides full details of a manager's true style orientation. **Table 2** shows a breakdown of a value manager's portfolio. This manager had positive exposure to B/P, dividend yield, earnings yield, cash flow, and S/P. Paradoxically, this manager also had positive exposure to some growth factors (ROE, earnings growth, and income to sales) and negative exposure to size, beta, and momentum. These tilts could have been a consequence of sector imbalances, so we adjusted for sectors. We found to our satisfaction that the growth features turned negative, so this manager had a consistent value orientation at this level. In fact, no systematic position can be seen in the growth category at all.

But something else started to jump out with this analysis; the portfolio exhibited high B/P, high dividend yield, high cash flow yield, and high sales to price but conspicuously low earnings yield. We approached some of the managers of the accounts and asked why they were low on earnings yield, because earnings yield is a significant value criterion.

[2] See Mr. Bernstein and Mr. Tupper's presentation, pp. 27–44.

Table 1. International Style Outlook

Country	Value: Standard	Value: Sector Adjusted (if different)	Growth: Standard	Growth: Sector Adjusted (if different)	Size: Standard	Size: Sector Adjusted (if different)
France	+		–		–	
Germany	+		↘	0	–	
Japan	–		+		–	
Singapore	+	↗	0		↗	
United Kingdom	↗		+		–	
United States	↗		↘		0	

Note: +/– = Predominantly positive/negative returns from the principal criteria for that style.
0 = Either no discernible trend, or the principal criteria for that style are in conflict.
↗↘ = Indications that the style return pattern is turning positive/negative.

Source: Global Style Advisor (London: Style Investment Research Associates, October 1997).

Their answer was that they knew from previous market analyses that the ability to recognize earnings is important, so they would rather try to forecast earnings yield than take it on faith and simply buy companies with high earnings yield. The evidence of the low position on earnings yield indicates that the manager is actually trying to forecast earnings. This finding reveals something about the manager and the firm's investment practices and philosophy that is typical of many value managers.

Table 2. Standard Deviations from Market Mean for a Value Manager's Standard and Sector-Adjusted Portfolio

Characteristic	Standard	Sector-Adjusted
B/P	0.8	0.8
Dividend yield	0.8	0.9
Earnings yield	0.3	0.1
Cash flow yield	0.7	0.8
S/P	0.3	0.4
ROE	0.0	0.0
Earnings growth	0.2	0.0
Income/sales	0.1	–0.2
Sales growth	0.0	–0.1
Market capitalization	–0.4	–0.3
Market beta	–0.3	–0.3
Historical relative performance	–0.5	–0.6
Debt/equity	–0.1	0.0
Foreign sales	–0.2	–0.2

Conclusion

Style is relevant, meaningful, and important in the vast majority of non-U.S. equity markets, but investors have to conduct style analysis in a way that is culturally sensitive to local markets. The timing of the performance patterns and nuances of style vary from market to market, and oversimplification risks rendering the concept inapplicable, possibly totally irrelevant, and most certainly unrewarding.

Properly applied style analysis reveals rich detail about market performance trends, market structure, and investor practices. But, as is often the case in non-U.S. environments, if portfolio managers do not listen carefully, they might not hear anything but noise.

Question and Answer Session

Robert Schwob

Question: Would you consider investment sectors as styles?

Schwob: Yes, but in the extended sense of style. I like to think of "style" as a very broad term, one that applies to any situation where the use of the concept results in a clear and justifiable partitioning of the market and a reduction in the vast amount of data necessary to perform equity analysis and portfolio management.

For example, defining groups of stocks according to arbitrary criteria results only in a multiplicity of categories, with no effective partitioning in the performance characteristics of any one group against any other. Consequently, there is no simplification gain. But identified "performance clusters" of shares do define relevant styles because each style can be managed against the other styles and can also be managed separately. The overall job of management has been effectively partitioned and, in a way, simplified, through the reduction in complexity, so we can analyze groups of stocks rather than each individual stock. Because industrial sectors tend to define performance clusters, sectors are not independent of style; they are interrelated.

Question: Is the regularity of the U.S. market a function of its superior efficiency?

Schwob: Yes. The statistics show a regular payoff pattern, which is usually evidence that the market is not efficient because it says that any recognizable pattern forms a profitable investment program. Our statistical analysis of the market, however, indicates that the market is efficient, but it is not efficient in the strong sense.

Style Investment Research Associates defines and reports on a particular statistic that measures the three- and six-month "mean aversion" or "mean reversion" of each factor-reward pattern reviewed. In the United States, these statistics, which we call "regularity" statistics, show that over a three- to six-month period, most of the major value factors are erratic and consequently virtually impossible to forecast, meaning that the market is very likely "weak-form efficient" with respect to the value cycle over the short term. Over longer periods, and with a bit of common sense thrown in, we believe that one can forecast styles, even in the United States, which must mean that we contend that the market is not "strong-form efficient."

Question: Could you use your Monte Carlo technique and the style framework to run a country- or sector-based hedge fund?

Schwob: The Monte Carlo technique, as we apply it, enables us to detect genuine styles and style factors within equity markets. Once a genuine style or performance cluster has been identified, the decision whether or not to manage it must be dependent on how successfully one believes one can manage the style and how one believes successful management might influence overall performance. We provide analysis on each style factor that will assist in answering these questions; this work takes us a bit beyond the identity issue of relevance, but it's still very accessible. Our regularity statistic helps to identify those factors that are most likely to be successfully managed using formal modeling techniques, and our attribution statistic identifies those factors that are most important to get right from a performance point of view.

Question: Does the impact of sector adjustment depend on whether the market is developed or emerging, large or small, or how the market is correlated with the U.S. market?

Schwob: The impact of sector adjustment depends on how unbalanced the sector concentrations are within the style portfolios and also how differently these poorly distributed sectors perform from the rest of the market. Generally, the larger, developed, and industrially balanced markets are less affected by sector adjustment than the smaller markets or those markets where specific large industrial sectors stand out in terms of size, performance trends, and financial ratios. Of course, that statement does imply strong sector-adjustment effects for emerging markets, but the same could also be said for a number of large and mid-sized markets.

Question: Does the Asian currency crisis affect sector-adjusted analysis and the ability to identify a manager's bias toward value or growth?

Schwob: Without sector adjustment, the style-reward patterns across most of Southeast Asia are extremely exaggerated, reflecting the sharply divergent performance of financial sectors and, very often, consumer stocks as well. Sector adjustment accounts for the exaggerated returns and usually smoothes them out, but often, as in Singapore and Australia, sector adjustment then causes the identity and overall relevance of the styles to drop dramatically—signifying that they were really only industry effects after all. In these markets, the recent crisis has made us very aware that, although portfolio analysis might reveal clear style tilts in Asian portfolios, these tilts may not be particularly relevant for analytical purposes; perhaps the only styles that genuinely matter are the industrial sectors themselves and positions in large market-dominating companies. But this information is also worthwhile.

Investing in Asia ex-Japan

Donald M. Krueger, CFA
Senior Managing Director
Valenzuela Capital Partners, Inc.

Volatility in Asian ex-Japan markets creates opportunity for the patient investor to provide liquidity to despondent sellers. Success in these markets requires identifying the necessary conditions in which to trade, implementing rules to ensure adequate liquidity and diversification, and executing strategic hedges (for example, out-of-the-money put options on stressed markets). A disciplined approach to investing—consistent application of simple business rules—needs time to work; therefore, patience is indeed a virtue in these markets.

Asia ex-Japan is a wide universe in which to hunt for the best companies that will make money for clients in the long term. This universe contains more than 2,000 listed companies—about the same size as the U.S. mid-capitalization market. It is a very wide and deep market with a wide range of investment choices. Unlike the G–7-type economies, which experience about 2–3 percent annual growth, Asian economies are growing rapidly, averaging about 5–10 percent annual growth, even if it sometimes dips negative. Because these economies are growing rapidly, they should be able to generate superior long-term earnings growth compared with the G–7 countries. The Asian ex-Japan economies always have a lot of activity, and that activity and volatility create opportunity. The combination of earnings growth and good valuation in this region is very exciting.

This presentation reviews the investment process that I have spent 20 years developing to manage the Pan Asia Fund, an Asian ex-Japan hedge fund. The process is one that works for me and one about which I feel very comfortable.

Investment Strategy

The investment strategy that I use has four main components. The process involves identifying the necessary conditions to trade, dealing with liquidity and diversification issues, executing strategic hedges during certain economic environments, and finally, exercising patience and discipline. Investing in Asia ex-Japan is not for the faint of heart or for those who want to be in and out of markets quickly.

Three Necessary Conditions

A company must meet three "necessary conditions" before I will consider adding it to my portfolio. These conditions may seem obvious, but in fact, all too often investors overlook them. When the fundamentals can be analyzed, when the valuations are attractive, and when identifiable catalysts are present, only then will I add the company to the portfolio.

First, I look only at companies whose fundamentals can be analyzed. Many companies have convoluted holding structures with strange capital structures that I cannot understand. If I cannot analyze the fundamentals, I am not going to invest in the company. I must also to be able to understand the fundamental business risks and opportunities of the company. The second condition is an attractive valuation. Analyzing a company's fundamentals is not sufficient. The valuation also must be attractive. The third condition is that an identifiable catalyst has to exist—one that will affect a company's value. Without an identifiable catalyst, I cannot put a company into my portfolio, even if the fundamentals can be analyzed and the valuation is attractive.

Fundamentals. The ability to analyze a company's fundamentals is critical. I must understand the business and its risks. I want to sit down and talk with the company's managers and make sure that they exist in the flesh. I often visit the plant to make sure the company actually has a building and that its inventory is not piled up to the sky. My associates and I visit more than 250 companies a year, after screening about 2,000. Although I am located in New

York, I am in Asia six to eight times a year. I do a lot of work with the company managers. If I have a question about the company, I want to be able to contact the managers and get an answer. We also calibrate the managers in terms of their ability and their integrity.

I must also be able to trust the financial data that I receive from a company. I need to know that the auditor is not the brother-in-law of the company president or that if the president has a private company that is delivering coal to fuel the plant, at least it supplies coal at reasonable prices. Having access to that type of corporate information is essential. If it is not available, stay away. A company's financials must be transparent.

Having been in the business for 20 years, I have a huge inventory of templates that I can use when I look at individual companies. If I understand the business risk and the business opportunities, then I feel comfortable. Too often young analysts, who have not covered more than two or three industries in their careers, will think they understand a potential investment. Often, they do not. They will make investment errors. Understanding the company businesses, opportunities, and risks is crucial.

Valuation. Valuation is the core of my investment process. I might find a company that is attractive fundamentally, but I have to determine what it is worth before I can decide whether I want to own it. John Templeton, one of the world's great investors, taught me to keep the process simple. John Templeton worked in the Bahamas thousands of miles away from some of the markets he invested in. His investment process involved determining what a company could earn over a five-year period. If it was trading at less than four times what the company could earn, he would consider buying it. If it was trading at more than eight times what the company could earn, then he would consider selling it. He had simple investment parameters and rules. But with those simple investment rules, he was able to manage complex portfolios across many industries and countries and do it successfully over the long term. Why? Because these simple rules are simple common sense, or as he said, "Common sense just is not that common any more." He is still right.

I have developed a number of commonsense valuation decision rules and parameters that incorporate several obvious criteria. To value a company, I use a model of earnings growth and local costs of capital. It is a simple procedure. **Figure 1** shows how

Figure 1. The Investment Strategy, Pan Asia Fund

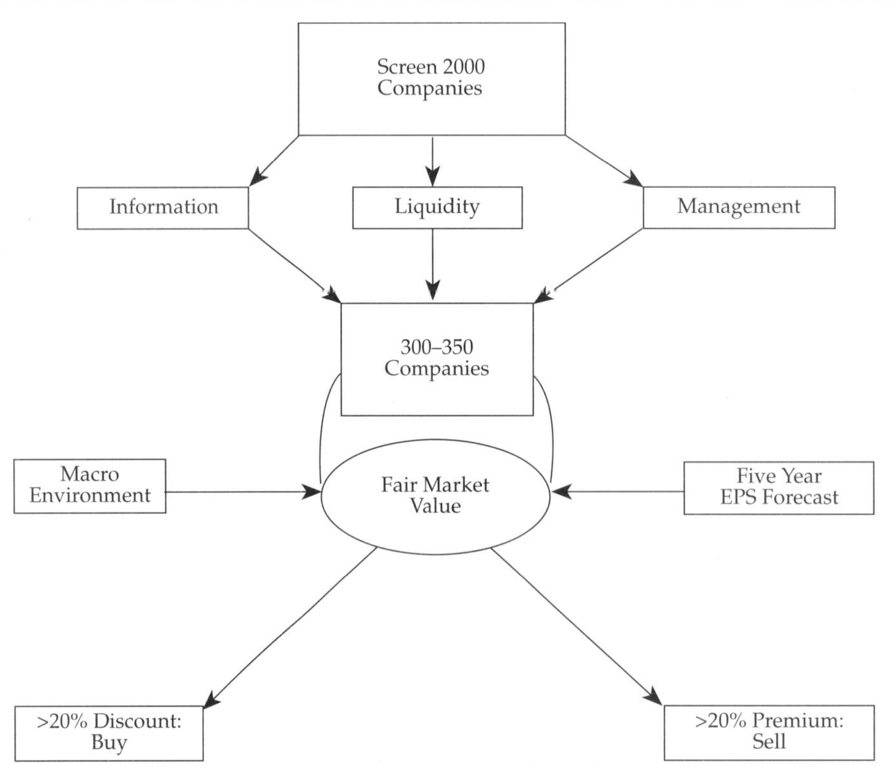

I calculate the fair market value for a company. My decision rule is to buy companies that trade at a 20 percent discount to the fair market value and to sell companies that trade at a 20 percent premium to fair market value. I leverage stocks, or consider leveraging them, when they are priced at large discounts to their fair market values, for example, 40 percent discounts. Also, I consider shorting stocks when they are priced at 40 percent premiums to fair market values.

These decision rules are simple, but if practiced consistently, they can result in superior investment performance. Again, my strategy is a simple, commonsense approach to the investment process.

In order to determine a company's fair market value, I first estimate what a company can earn over a normalized five-year time period. I then make an earnings projection based on what I think normalized earnings will be five years from now. I make the five-year earnings estimate based on my discussions with management, my understanding of the industry, the financials of the company, and other such factors. Twenty years of experience tells me to assume earnings will never increase after this five-year period, because the future is so uncertain. Based on that approach and an earnings discount model, I can determine the fair market value.

The discount rate for every country in which I invest is generally a function of sovereign risk and inflation. By combining my Year 5 EPS estimate and the discount rate, I calculate the present value (PV) of the Year 5 EPS using the formula provided in **Figure 2**. Then I calculate what I call the "fair-market-value prime," which values the PV of Year 5 EPS as a perpetual instrument. I discount the value of this perpetuity by a discount rate that takes into consideration the combination of sovereign risk and normalized inflation rate. This discount rate changes over time. For example, before the August 1997 currency crisis, I used an 11 percent discount rate for Indonesia; now I use a 15 percent discount rate because of the recent volatility there. Finally, I add the PV of the dividend stream for that five-year period to the PV of the perpetuity after the five-year period to get the fair market value.

Every investment style has to have some type of fair-market-value anchor. No matter how it is done, in general, an investor must have some sense of knowing whether a stock is expensive or cheap. Fair market value can be calculated in many ways—price-to-book ratio, P/E, price-to-cash flow ratio, dividend discount models—as long as some kind of consistent approach is used.

Figure 2. Determining Fair Market Value

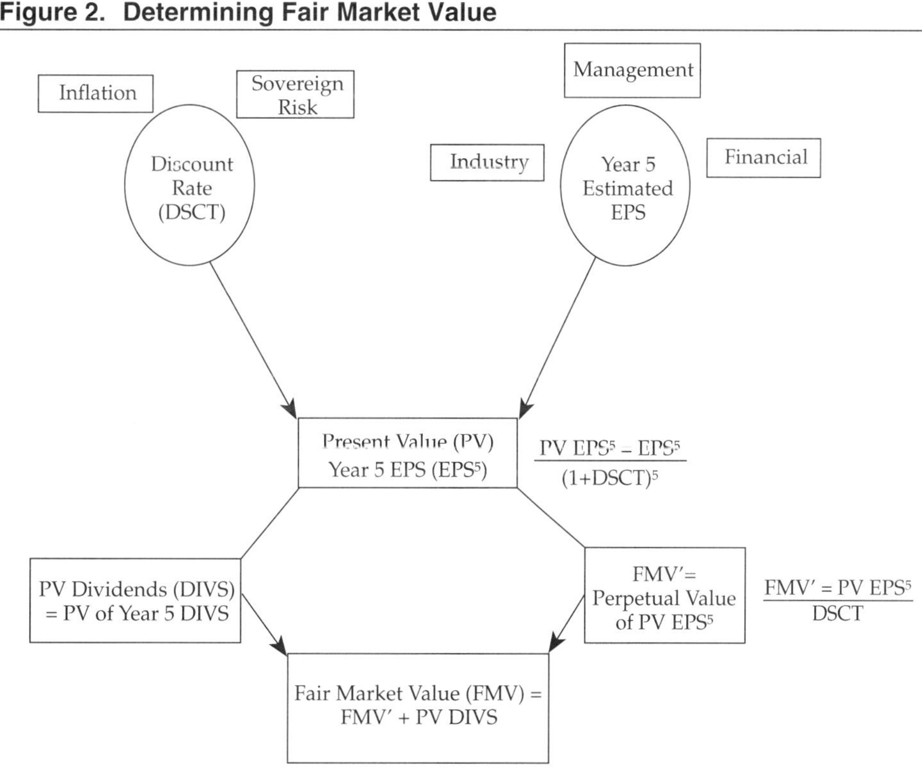

Note: FMV′ assumes level growth in EPS after Year 5.

In summary, I use a valuation template to analyze companies that interest me. I have used this template for many markets, even in today's U.S. and European markets. For every company, I calculate a fair market value, a buy target, and a sell target. I look at the current price relative to the fair market value, the projected buy price relative to the current price, and the sell price relative to the current price. This approach simply uses a normalized earnings value and applies a discount rate to it—that is, it treats normalized earnings like a perpetual security. This approach provides some sense of fair market value.

Catalyst. The third necessary condition is that I must be able to identify some catalyst that will result in a re-rating of the company. Many fundamentally attractive companies sell at very inexpensive valuations, but they are ones that will always sell at very inexpensive valuations. Unless I can identify the catalysts for change, I stay away from them. Typically, if I am looking at a group of companies that have strong fundamentals and attractive valuations, I will buy the companies with the most distinct catalysts that have the highest likelihood of upward revaluations and short the companies with the most distinct negative catalysts and the highest likelihood of downward revaluations. This step is a necessary part of the investment process. The three parameters, the three necessary conditions—attractive fundamentals, attractive valuations, and identifiable catalysts—all must be met before companies go into my portfolio.

Liquidity

Liquidity is a major concern in these markets. I have lost money by investing in illiquid stocks and then being unable to trade them when clients wanted out. I am so paranoid about the process that the Pan Asia Fund is probably one of the few hedge funds that invests in Asia and is willing to give clients monthly liquidity, because I know that I can liquidate every company I have in the portfolio within 15 trading days. The portfolio is restricted from owning more than 10 percent of any security's free float and more than 10 days of the average trading volume for any security. These figures are monitored carefully. In times when markets absolutely break down, the rules have to bend a little because liquidity totally dries up. We include *force majeure* in our offering memorandum to protect us from any serious problems, but except for those three or four times every five years (and 1997 happens to be one of those times), the liquidity of the fund's holdings is adequate and we have no problem whatsoever meeting those parameters.

Diversification

When investing in Asia, having a diversified portfolio is essential, and being a little paranoid is also helpful. The reason is that most of these markets do not have the kind of government oversight and government protection (perhaps excluding Singapore) that exists in the more developed markets around the world. The SEC regulators in the United States have eyes in the backs of their heads and can catch companies doing almost anything. The same cannot be said about the regulatory authorities in Asia.

Owners of Asian companies tend to have an "indifferent attitude" toward minority shareholders. Many of the company managements have their private placements. They raise funds from their public offerings but live off their private vehicles. When they see the foreigners coming, they start to laugh. Therefore, I have to be aware of the high probability of what I call "company surprises." Any company in this part of the world is more likely to blow up and have a company surprise than a company in an environment such as the United States, where if a company's management did some of the things that Asian managements did, the regulatory authorities would be looking over their shoulders or management would be going to jail. Perhaps I am cynical and paranoid, but I have seen time and again that it pays to be cynical and paranoid.

Having several useful diversification rules in these markets is also helpful. The universe for the Pan Asia Fund portfolio ex-Japan encompasses everything from Australia through the Indian subcontinent. In order to manage a reasonably diversified portfolio, I invest in at least five countries throughout the region. The maximum investment in any one country is 35 percent of the portfolio's assets. This rule helped protect me from the October 1997 blowup in Hong Kong because I did not have more than 35 percent of my assets there. So, rather than use Hong Kong as a safe haven and invest 60 percent of my assets there, I capped out at a much lower level. My maximum investment in any one company is 7 percent of the portfolio's assets, and I rarely, if ever, have 7 percent in one company because that is too concentrated, given the possibility, or indeed the probability, of company surprises.

Strategic Hedges

Strategic hedges should be used carefully. Although I run a hedge fund, I primarily use strategic hedges to protect the equity portfolio when markets experience stress, rather than to enhance returns.

The problem that investors face is that the best times to buy undervalued securities are at points of "maximum pessimism." But these are also the times when protection is needed the most. If I can hedge my holdings in troubled markets, then I can be reasonably comfortable buying stocks in those markets. Furthermore, I can be the provider of liquidity to despondent sellers. I traditionally construct hedges by purchasing out-of-the-money puts in the market when things are fine, when volatility is low and the puts are quite inexpensive. My hope is that those puts will expire worthless—that I will have paid an insurance premium and it expires worthless. As with life insurance, people want to pay their premiums; they do not want to die and win. Similarly, in these markets, I pay my insurance premiums, but I do not want to die and win. If the market suffers a cataclysm, I can protect the integrity of the portfolio and continue to practice my strategy: leverage up the portfolio, buy when others are despondently selling, and take advantage of some of the best valuations in the market.

Patience and Discipline

Patience and discipline are essential components of my investment strategy. Patience means many things, but primarily, patience means minimizing portfolio turnover. I do not necessarily want to make brokers rich, and the transaction costs in these markets can be very high. Not only are commissions high, but bid–ask spreads also can be 20 percent. Some might say that level of spread is unconscionable, but that is business. Congratulations to the brokers, but I do not necessarily want to be the one who enriches them.

Investors have to be vigilant of the high transaction costs associated with trading securities in Asia. When I was a portfolio manager at another company, we conducted a study that found that the transaction costs ex-commissions were often about 15 percent for a one-way trade and in some cases as high as about 30 percent. I try to limit my trading and keep annual portfolio turnover to less than 50 percent. For a hedge fund, that turnover rate is considered low. In fact, my turnover has been somewhat less than 50 percent because I want to be a bottom-up value investor: select stocks based on the fundamentals, the valuations, and the catalysts and allow the investment process to work.

Investors have to exercise discipline, no matter what market they are in. For example, even though I am hedged right now and I am buying, I feel it in my stomach that the market is headed down. Nevertheless, I know how my investment discipline works, and I must stick with it. I know when it is time to buy a stock. I know when it is time to sell a stock. I know when it is time to short a stock. I know when it is time to leverage a stock. All I have to do is maintain the disciplined approach to investing that I have applied during the past 20 years; it seems to work.

Summary

My investment process is built on commonsense principles. I screen 2,000 companies based on various information, such as the liquidity of the stock and the management of the company. That screening reduces the universe to about 300–350 companies that I can comfortably analyze. I calculate the fair market value of those 300–350 companies based on the five-year EPS forecast and the macro environment. When companies trade at 20 percent discounts, they become candidates for purchase. When they trade at 20 percent premiums, they become candidates for sale. If the catalysts are right, then I actually act on those buy and sell rules, but all the while I must consider strategic hedges to protect me from the market. The Pan Asia Fund is only about 1.5 years old, so I do not have a long-established track record with the fund, but so far, I have been able to deliver returns at least 500 basis points (bps) above the benchmark. Thus, this strategy works well for me and is one that I am comfortable with, but I cannot say whether it is the right strategy for all investors to use.

Question and Answer Session

Donald M. Krueger, CFA

Question: How long do you wait for a catalyst for a potential investment?

Krueger: Generally, I am willing to let something evolve and develop for 12–18 months. Although I use a five-year normalized earnings growth rate when I am making my calculations for fair market value, the catalyst itself should be much shorter than that. I do not want to have dead money in the portfolio for more than 12–18 months; even 18 months is pushing it a little.

Question: How do you forecast five years of EPS growth and dividends for companies in Asia?

Krueger: My forecasts are based on experience and the history of the companies—their balance sheets, the industries that they are in, etc. It is not a very precise process. For example, I will look at a company, such as a bank, and if I see the bank is earning a 30 percent return on equity (ROE), I will simply say that is not sustainable. Over long periods of time, banks in the region are probably more capable of having ROEs of 18–20 percent, or perhaps even lower. So, I consider that ROE of 30 percent at that particular bank as too high. Therefore, I need to make an adjustment. I normalize earnings from the base period. Over time, these banks cannot generate 40 percent earnings growth a year, as they have; a realistic annual earnings growth is perhaps more like 12.5 percent to 15 percent. I try to make fairly conservative assumptions. With those conservative assumptions about ROE and growth, I cap the fair market value on discount rates and assume that earnings can never grow after Year 5. I try to err on the side of conservatism. Science isn't really involved in my forecasts. They are based on experience and accounting adjustments.

Question: How do you determine the specific limits for your diversification rules?

Krueger: Again, my diversification limits are based on experience.

Question: What kind of mistakes have you made over the years, and what have you learned from them?

Krueger: I have learned that all too often I have thought I had an edge, that I understood management. I thought that they were my buddies—they would phone me at night and tell me what was going on—only to find out that was not the case.

The same goes for the macro situations. Economies can blow up overnight. For example, I had no idea that the Indonesian economy was going to blow up. I had no idea that the Philippines economy was going to blow up. I was shocked the last two weeks in August 1997, and my portfolio reflected that. I had not put on any hedges for those markets. I was hedged at that time in Thailand and Malaysia, but I did not have a specific hedge in Indonesia and the Philippines. Fortunately, my decision rules saved me. Diversification limits—7 percent on individual companies and 35 percent on individual countries—kept me, more than anything else, from making tragic mistakes with the overall portfolio. These rules are really to protect me from myself more than anything else.

Question: Would a highly quantitative approach to Asian equity investments be effective?

Krueger: I would suggest that at this point in the evolution of these Asian markets, it would be premature to get too quantitative. You find too many inconsistencies. You need too many dummy variables. You would have too many spurious correlations. I would say to wait a few years. Let the markets get a little more efficient before you get too quantitative, and in the meantime, practice the art of stock picking and investing.

Question: What would you consider an appropriate benchmark of Asia ex-Japan portfolios?

Krueger: It should be whatever benchmark works for you. In my case, I use the Morgan Stanley Capital International Asia Pacific Free ex-Japan Index because it is easy for me to call up on Bloomberg and it is a respected benchmark, but other indexes exist. I also look at the Lipper indexes for Asia ex-Japan and at some of the databases of other hedge fund managers. So, I actually use several benchmarks.

Question: Would you buy out-of-the-money puts when the implied volatility is extremely high and the spreads are sensational?

Krueger: I buy out-of-the-money puts when markets are calm and tranquil and hope that on rocky days I already own them and they are deep in the money. When the markets are under stress, I sell futures. For example, I am shorting Malaysian futures as an umbrella for the Association of South East

Asian Nations markets. They are liquid; I am able to get hold of them; and I do not have to worry about dealing with the OTC market. They are not perfect hedges, but if I buy them, they can help me hedge against not only Malaysia but also the Philippines and Indonesia. All these countries have faced the same kind of systematic currency problems and the same systematic meltdown of their economies.

Question: Do you hedge currencies?

Krueger: Most of the time, not explicitly. In my strategic hedges, currency hedging is explicit because the hedges that I use are generally composite options, which include both currency and market hedges. Conceptually, the cost of capital that I use should, over a long time, reflect the differential inflation rates among the different countries. For example, if I am looking at Indonesia right now and I believe Indonesia will have 11 percent inflation on a normalized basis over the next five years as a result of the recent currency devaluation and its sovereign risk is high, then I will use a 16 percent discount rate. If the cost of capital that I use for Singapore is 8 percent, a 800 bps difference exists between the two. Companies that cannot meet my criteria for investing in Indonesia would easily meet those criteria in Singapore. In other words, companies have to be much more "discounted" in Indonesia in order for me to buy them for the portfolio. They have to have much more appreciation potential in their local currencies that would translate into an attractive Singapore dollar-based return than a Singapore company would have to have. So, currency hedges are captured by the differentials in the cost of capital that I use.

Question: Would you call yourself a value or a growth investor?

Krueger: I call myself a stock picker, but if pressed, I would probably call myself a value stock picker rather than a growth stock picker. Basically, I am skeptical about growth stocks. I do not believe that many companies can grow their earnings at 60 percent a year for five years, which is the criteria I use in my valuation models. If you look at the types of companies that I have in my portfolio, you can see that they are not true "growth" companies.

Let me give you a good example—"red chips" (i.e., shares of Chinese government-related companies incorporated in Hong Kong). I short red chips. I do not go long red chips, and that decision affected my performance for a few months when red chips were sailing to wild valuations. As a value investor, I could not find value in the red chips. Investors really had to pin a lot of hopes on the growth premiums embedded in the share prices, and no one knew how long those premiums would last. Red chips are similar to the old 1920s blind pools and the 1960s-style conglomerates that existed in the United States, most of which were discredited and collapsed. Now, we are seeing the collapse of the red chips. Maybe red chips will survive; China is different from the United States. Maybe red-chip managers know how to manage throngs of companies in a conglomerate form, and perhaps, the investors really are smart enough to take up a blind pool and add value, but as a value investor, I cannot find the value in red chips. Maybe I would as a growth investor if I believed in the concept.

Currency Management in Asian Equity Portfolios

Michael C.M. Wilson
Vice President
J.P. Morgan & Company, Inc.

High volatility in Asian currency markets is here to stay. Because the correlation between Asian foreign exchange and equity markets is very low—almost nonexistent—systematic hedging of all Asian currency exposure is not a good solution and will not reduce the volatility of returns. Tactical hedging is a more appropriate strategy, and various analytical approaches are available to help investors make their hedging decisions.

In 1997, currency markets in Asia were incredibly volatile—especially from May 1997 forward—which poses interesting long-term challenges for equity managers. Major movements in the Thai baht, Indonesian rupiah, and Malaysian ringgit had spill-over effects on Asian equity markets in 1997. Clearly, the increased volatility in Asian currency markets illustrates the importance of managing currency risk in Asian equity portfolios.

In this presentation, I will discuss how to apply currency approaches to equity portfolios, particularly those affected by Asian emerging market currencies. Specifically, I will cover four issues: historical use of currency hedging, the importance of currency hedging in the future, characteristics of emerging Asian currency markets, and analytical methods available to help make the hedging decision.

Historical Perspective

In the past, investors had three good reasons for not hedging Asian emerging market equity portfolios. First, the currencies had a very high dollar component. Most analysts look at returns in U.S. dollar terms, so paying to hedge something that was essentially linked to, or pegged against, the U.S. dollar did not make much sense. Second, hedging was expensive. Either very high interest rates in Asian emerging countries significantly increased hedging costs, or the currencies, such as the Singapore dollar, were typically appreciating. Third is the issue of coincident fundamentals. Many fund managers say, "If I am bullish on the Indonesian equity market, I am also bullish on the currency. Because hedging would imply that I have a different view on the currency than I have on the stock market, why bother hedging?"

Historically, the decision not to hedge was the right one most of the time because currency movements had a negligible effect on cumulative total returns and the volatility of returns. As **Figure 1** shows, the difference between unhedged and hedged cumulative total equity market returns was not large during the 1992–96 period. If an investor was in the right market, hedging the currency exposure did not matter. In most markets, one of the objectives of currency hedging is to dampen volatility. But currency hedging has had a negligible impact in terms of volatility in the Asian equity markets.

Future Perspective

The old world of relatively stable currencies against the U.S. dollar is gone, and greater volatility is here to stay. Clearly, the link to the dollar has gone with the exception of a few markets: the Hong Kong dollar and to some extent the Chinese renminbi. The Thai baht's float triggered currency contagion in Asia, which significantly increased the volatility of Asian currencies. After July 1, 1997, many Asian currencies moved dramatically relative to the U.S. dollar. For example, the Thai baht fell 18 percent after float; the Indonesian rupiah fell 5.89 percent after the intervention band widened from 8.0 percent to 12.0 percent, and the Philippine peso fell by 12 percent after its foreign exchange regime was relaxed. These currency movements were the largest foreign exchange

Figure 1. Total Returns and Volatility of Quarterly Returns for Various Asian Markets, 1992–96

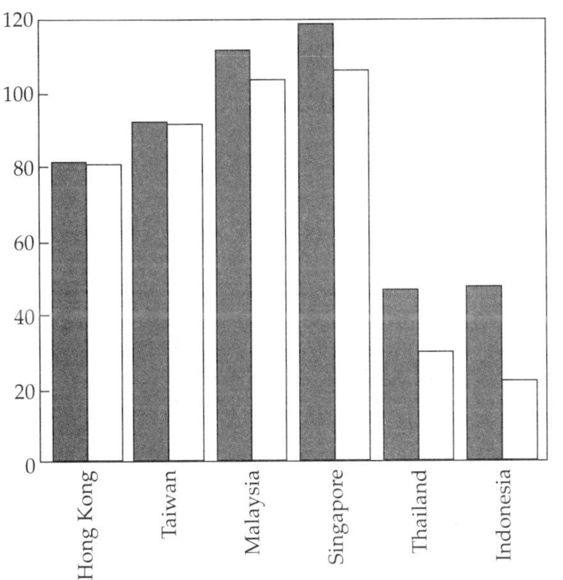

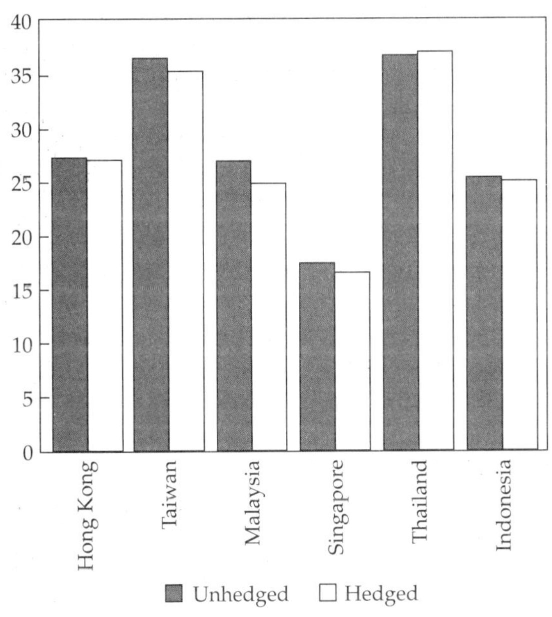

moves to take place during the preceding five years; however, foreign exchange rates have made even larger moves since September 1997.

Comparing the volatility of Asian currency, bond, and equity markets with those of G–7 countries provides an interesting perspective from which to make future predictions.

G–7 Currency Comparisons. One way of looking at foreign exchange volatility is to examine daily changes against the U.S. dollar. Before May 1997, daily foreign exchange rates changed very little. Since then, foreign exchange movements have oscillated in a much wider band, and this pattern is likely to continue. The big question is, what will be the likely volatility in Asian currencies one year forward? Historically, the volatility of the dollar/yen and dollar/mark rates has typically been 10–12 percent; most of the Asian currencies' foreign exchange rates against the dollar had exhibited about 1 or 2 percent volatility. When the current bout of volatility subsides, the volatility of Asian exchange rates will probably settle somewhere in the region of 8–10 percent. Asian exchange rates certainly will not be at current levels, which during the past six months amounted to about 30 percent or more for the Malaysian ringgit, the Indonesian rupiah, and the Thai baht.

G–7 Bond Market Comparisons. Historical volatility and return patterns for G–7 bond markets can help managers make the hedging decision for Asian equity markets. Consider the bond markets. During the 1992–97 period, the average U.S. dollar returns for hedged and unhedged G–7 bond investments did not change significantly, and the average cost of hedging was nearly flat for that whole time frame. **Table 1** shows that if U.S. dollar-based investors had invested in Japanese bonds, they would have achieved an annual return of 10.8 percent in dollars, or about 0.9 percent a month. The annualized volatility of an unhedged investment ranged from 1.20 to 3.65 percent. If the investor had used one-month rolling hedges to hedge the currency exposure, the average return would not have changed significantly. The big difference is in the volatility. Hedging significantly reduced volatility in all of the markets listed in Table 1. Indeed, the volatility is roughly the same order of magnitude as investing only in unhedged U.S. bonds. This reduction in volatility explains why the majority of bond market investors use currency overlay programs. By separating the currency and the bond market decisions, investors can focus on bond market values and reduce volatility by hedging; the currency overlay specialists can determine where to extract value from currency markets.

G–7 Equity Market Comparisons. The equity markets tell a different story. According to Table 1, the average returns for the hedged and unhedged investments are very similar, as with the bond markets. The volatility of equity returns, however, unlike bond markets, is not significantly affected by hedging. Systematic hedging of currency exposures across G–7 equity markets does not reduce volatility the same way it does with G–7 bond markets because foreign exchange returns in G–7 countries are less

Table 1. Average Monthly U.S. Dollar Returns and Annual Volatility for Various G–7 Markets, May 1992–August 1997

	Unhedged		Hedged		
Market	Average Return	Volatility	Average Return	Volatility	Correlation[a]
Bond					
Japan	0.90%	3.65%	0.93%	1.41%	0.91%
Germany	0.65	2.91	0.67	1.03	0.94
United Kingdom	0.74	2.87	0.68	1.75	0.82
United States	0.60	1.20	na	na	na
Equity					
Japan	0.51%	6.76%	0.53%	5.71%	0.51%
Germany	1.08	4.22	1.16	4.81	0.15
United Kingdom	1.22	3.59	1.17	3.45	0.47
United States	1.26	2.95	na	na	na

na = not applicable.

[a]U.S. dollar unhedged/foreign exchange rate.

correlated with local equity market returns. As Table 1 shows, the correlation of foreign exchange movements with equity markets is significantly less than the correlation with bond markets.

The relationship between Asian foreign exchange returns and equity returns is almost nonexistent. As **Figure 2** shows, the correlation was close to zero before the 1997 currency crisis. In the high-dollar-content currency movement, little linkage is found between currency returns and stock market returns.

The G–7 markets present a slightly different picture. **Figure 3** shows that a correlation exists between local currency equity returns and foreign exchange returns in G–7 markets. A weakened currency helps the export industry, which is reflected in the local stock market valuation. Added competitiveness in export-oriented industries filters through to produce higher equity returns. This effect explains why systematic foreign exchange hedging of equity market returns is unlikely to reduce the volatility of returns in most markets.

Predictions. Based on historical evidence, several predictions can be made about the future of Asian emerging markets. First, currency volatility will likely remain. Second, Asian currencies will not revert back to semifixed positions against the U.S. dollar. Therefore, currency movements will affect the total returns of Asian equity portfolios, particularly when dollar-based returns are used. Third, if Asian markets follow the route of most of the G–7 markets, systematic hedging of all currency exposure is unlikely to be a good

Figure 2. Correlations of Foreign Exchange and Local Currency Equity Returns: Asia, 1992–96

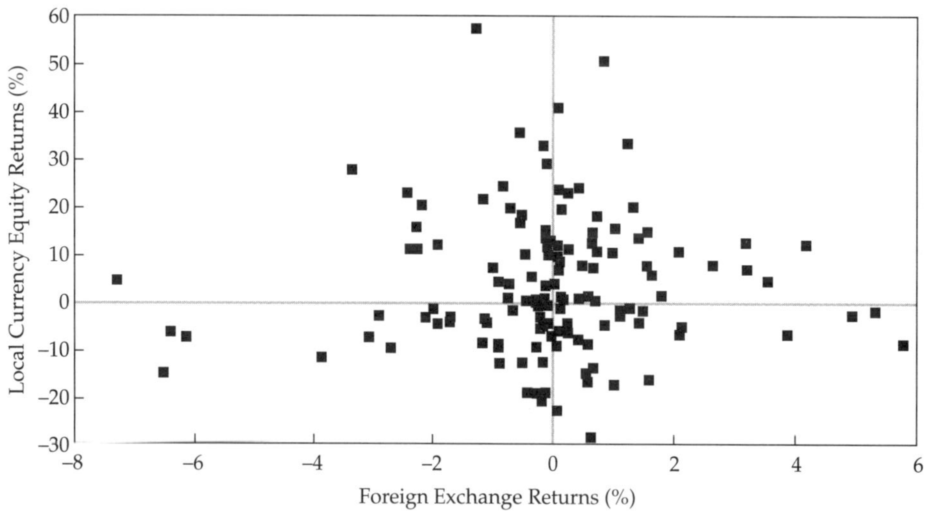

Figure 3. Correlations of Foreign Exchange and Local Currency Equity Returns: Germany and the United Kingdom, 1992–96

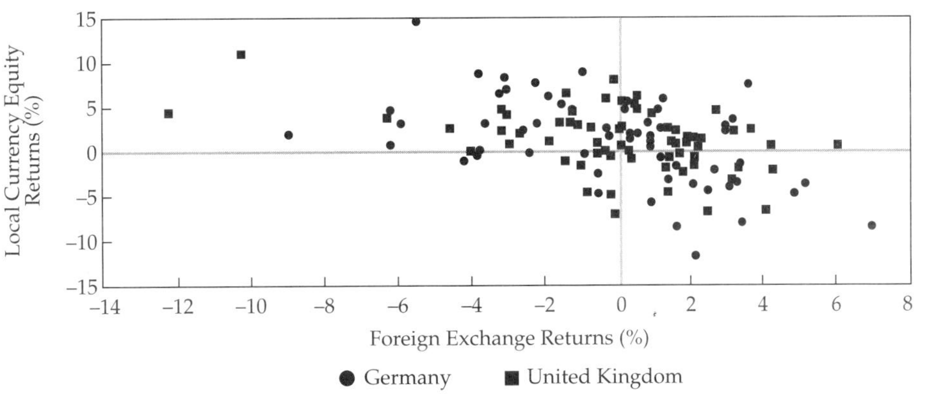

Local Currency Equity Returns (%)

Foreign Exchange Returns (%)

● Germany ■ United Kingdom

solution and will not reduce volatility. Instead, tactical hedging for particular situations—focusing on whether currency movements will detract from equity movements—will be much more appropriate.

Market Characteristics

With the added volatility in Asian markets, investors need to think about how to hedge selectively. The first step involves analyzing the hedging instruments available in the various markets. As **Table 2** shows, available hedging instruments provide an indicator of market liquidity. A full arsenal of G–7 instruments is available but with different levels of liquidity. Hong Kong has by far the most liquid market, particularly in the case of swaps; Hong Kong's swap market is liquid and well traded out to 10 years. Indonesia, Malaysia, and Thailand follow behind Hong Kong in terms of market liquidity and openness. Their foreign exchange markets are completely open, and the turnover per day is significant. Some of their swap markets are reasonably liquid out to 5 years and can be negotiated out to 10 years. At J.P. Morgan, our clients frequently use Indonesian, Malaysian, and Thai currency option markets.

Although Singapore has an open, liquid foreign exchange market, it also has restrictions on what can be done in the forward markets. Short-selling restrictions mean that currency options can be used to hedge only a fundamental underlying economic activity, which makes the option market relatively illiquid.

South Korea, the Philippines, Taiwan, China, and India provide even less liquidity and are essentially nondeliverable markets. The foreign exchange markets in these countries are not fully convertible and have local restrictions and special structure requirements. To construct currency hedges, investors often access offshore markets and purchase nondeliverable forward contracts. The strike price for a currency contract can be set using onshore levels, and the buyer agrees to pay the profit/loss in U.S. dollars based on some screen rate. No actual conversion of the underlying currency takes place, but the economic equivalent profit in U.S. dollars is paid or received, depending on currency moves.

Table 2. Hedging Instruments Available in Various Asian Markets

Instrument	Hong Kong	Indonesia	Malaysia	Thailand	Singapore	South Korea[a]	Philippines[a]	Taiwan[a]	China[a]	India[a]
Interest rate swaps	✔	✔	✔	✔	✔	✔	✔	✔		
Forward rate agreements	✔	✔	✔	✔	✔	✔	✔	✔		
Caps/floors	✔	✔	✔	✔	✔					
Swap options	✔	✔	✔	✔	✔					
Cross-currency swaps	✔	✔	✔	✔	✔	✔	✔	✔		
Forwards and swaps[b]	✔	✔	✔	✔	✔	✔	✔	✔	✔	✔
Foreign exchange options	✔	✔	✔	✔						

[a]Subject to local restrictions and special structures.
[b]Includes forwards, long-dated forwards, and swaps.

Investors usually hedge currency exposure into the U.S. dollar because they frequently measure returns in dollars and the dollar is the most liquid currency in terms of execution. The simplest way to determine the cost of hedging is to take the quoted interest rate in the local market and subtract the U.S. dollar interest rate. As **Table 3** shows, the annual cost of hedging different currency exposures into the U.S. dollar varies significantly. For example, with three-month interest rates in Thailand at 16.59 percent and three-month interest rates in the United States at 5.65 percent, hedging Thai equity exposure annually costs about 10.94 percent. In other words, if an investor had invested in the Thai stock market and had hedged the baht using three-month forward contracts, the end cost in U.S. dollars would have been close to 11 percent. Similarly, hedging the Indonesian rupiah into U.S. dollars annually costs about 14.35 percent. In contrast, if an investor had hedged yen or a Japanese equity portfolio back into U.S. dollars, the investor would have achieved an incremental 5 percent return because of very low interest rates in Japan—0.50 percent in Japan versus 5.65 percent in the United States.

Table 3. Interest Rates and Hedging Costs as of September 15, 1997

Currency	Three-Month Rates	Annual Hedging Cost
U.S. dollar	5.65%	—
German mark	3.24	–2.41%
Hong Kong dollar	7.48	1.83
Indonesian rupiah	20.00	14.35
Japanese yen	0.50	–5.15
Malaysian ringgit	8.07	2.42
Philippine peso	17.00	11.35
Singapore dollar	4.65	–1.00
Thai baht	16.59	10.94

Hedging costs can also be determined by looking at the cost in expression of the forward points, which is the way forward contracts are usually quoted. Most fund managers look at one- or three-month forward contracts when hedging currency exposure, but the problem of residual error arises. If a manager hedges forward a particular equity portfolio for one month, the manager does not know what the portfolio value will be at the end of the one-month period. When entering into a forward contract, the manager has to make some assumption of what the local currency or the dollar value will be at the end of the period and hedge that amount back into U.S. dollars. If any residual error exists on that final date, the manager either has to roll the contract by not actually making the underlying conversion or make an adjustment right at the end when the exact value is known.

Analytical Approaches

Various analytical approaches are available to help investors decide when to hedge currency risk. Individual investors not only have their own objectives for return and risk tolerance but also their own market views. Counterparties, such as J.P. Morgan, hope to influence those views, but at the end of the day, each investor needs to look at his or her own currency-hedging view.

When trying to decide whether to hedge currency exposure, as an investor, you must think about the following four factors.

- *Currency volatility.* If you expect the currency to be highly volatile during the next three months, you are much more likely to hedge that currency exposure.
- *Interest rate differentials.* High interest rate differentials indicate that it will cost a lot to hedge. So, all else being equal, you are less likely to want to hedge that exposure.
- *Currency trend.* If the currency has been depreciating significantly during the past four months or so and if you expect that trend to continue, you will be more concerned about currency hedging than if you thought the currency was likely to turn around and stabilize or appreciate.
- *Event risk.* If you believe that the currency will be devalued sharply, say a 20 percent move in one day, then you will be more likely to want to hedge the currency.

These factors are straightforward and are the same for G–7 or local emerging markets. But quantifying these factors is tough.

Break-even Standard Deviations. One approach we use, which was probably more relevant a year ago than now, is to analyze break-even standard deviations, as shown in **Figure 4** for the Indonesian rupiah. Based on the five-year history of the rupiah as of September 1996, we calculated the two-year trend (extrapolating out five years), measured the volatility during these two years, and drew a one-standard-deviation cone around the trend. The trend indicated that if history repeats, the chance that the rupiah will be within this band is about 67 percent. Finally, we assessed current market indications. At the time, one-year forward rates or break-even swap rates out to five years indicated that the market clearly expected a large movement in the rupiah. Figure 4 illustrates that the market had a substantially different view on the rupiah than the trend calculated with historical spot rates. In other words, the premium in September 2001, which is the difference in terms of standard deviations between the trend line and the forward rate, essentially represents a market risk premium for

Figure 4. Indonesian Rupiah Exchange Rate Risk, October 1991–September 2001

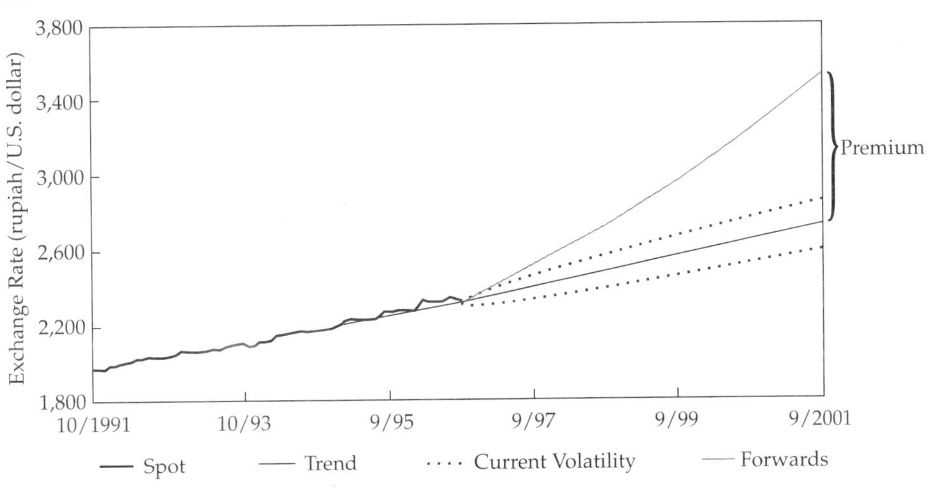

Note: Data measured as of September 24, 1996.

the chance that the rupiah would devalue. At that time, the expected size of the devaluation was quite large—about 9 or 10 standard deviations, and the mathematical probability of such a devaluation was relatively remote. Given that the market indicated a non-normal distribution for the rupiah, the market priced into forward rates a significant probability of a jump in the exchange rate.

As of August 1997, the market indicated a return to a more normal pattern, as **Figure 5** shows. The trend line has a much steeper slope than in Figure 4 because of the sharp jump in the exchange rate in August 1997. The volatility cone is significantly wider than in Figure 4 because the volatility of the currency has increased. Since September 1997, forward rates approximate the trend line, which is actually a coincidence but one would expect them to be somewhere within this wide volatility cone. Forward rates indicate that the market has already built in a repetition of the past, but they do not indicate an extra premium for a high chance of another big devaluation. Where this trend line is placed certainly makes this analysis more an art than a science. But applying this analysis across different markets gives a good measure of the amount of risk that is priced into the foreign exchange market and of the probability of sharp moves in different currencies.

Figure 5. Indonesian Rupiah Exchange Rate Risk, September 1992–August 2002

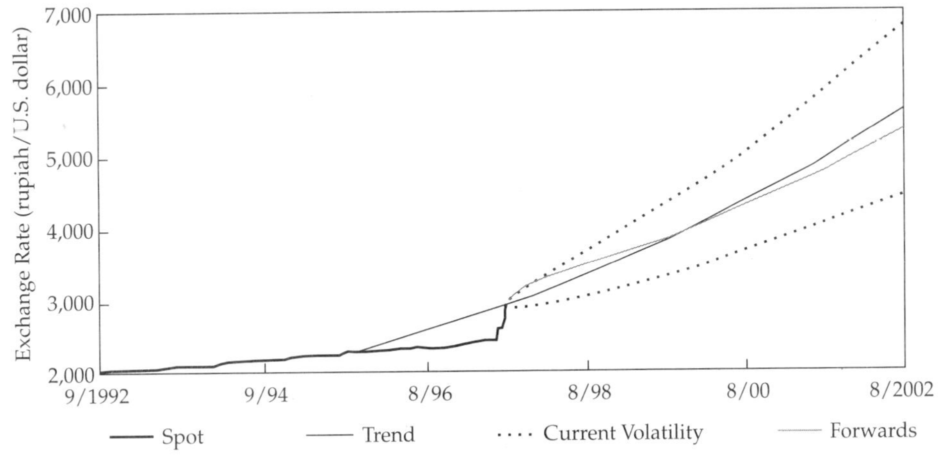

Note: Data measured as of August 28, 1997.

Break-even standard deviations can also be applied historically. For example, **Figure 6** uses one-year foreign exchange forwards for the Thai baht and indicates how many standard deviations the market prices in terms of event risk. Historically, 2.0–2.5 standard deviations, which was relatively high, was the average risk premium built into Thai baht forwards. Since the declining volatility in early 1997, the break-even standard deviation is within a one-standard-deviation band and has been for most of 1997, apart from the artificial two-tier market before the devaluation.

Quantifying Pressure on Foreign Exchange Rates. An alternative approach combines various market indicators to measure the relative pressure on exchange rates. Many investors talk about the amount of pressure on a foreign exchange market. Rather than trying to derive a measure that indicates what the currency will do tomorrow, we try to determine whether a lot of pressure exists on individual currencies and how that pressure compares across countries and time.

When a currency is under pressure, interest rates typically rise to defend the currency. Furthermore, the yield curve usually inverts because short-term rates are higher than long-term rates. So, short-term interest rate levels and the degree of yield curve inversion, measured as a percentage of prior levels, are built into this approach. We compare interest rates today with the average during all of the previous year to account for the structural differences between markets; expressing the difference as a percentage gives an indication of how high rates are. In terms of the yield curve, we look at the ratio of 1-month rates to 12-month rates.

Equity markets are a leading, or at least coincident, indicator of foreign capital leaving a market. But most of the economic data come out so late they are of limited use. So, the amount of change in the equity markets over the previous two weeks is built into this model. We also normalize the data. Because the U.S. stock market has such a significant impact on global stock markets, we factor out the U.S. change over that time period and look at the differential change between Asian markets over the past two weeks. We initially set this two-week differential equal to 100 percent. If it moves higher, it indicates that the currency is under more pressure, and if it goes lower, it is under less pressure.

The pressure on Asian emerging market currencies during much of 1997 has been high. As **Figure 7** shows, this measure has risen significantly during 1997 and was quite high in May and June when the Thai baht was under intense pressure. When the Thai baht was devalued (on July 3, 1997), pressure collapsed because of the fall from the artificially high rates. In July and August, as other currency turmoils unfolded, the pressure on Asian emerging currencies increased. In fact, on October 3, 1997, currency pressure was at 180 percent because of the high rates in Korea and Hong Kong and, to some extent, Singapore and Taiwan. For about the past two years up to early May 1997, this measure always ranged between 95 and 105 percent, moving within a very tight band.

This measure of currency pressure can be broken down to look at individual currencies. As **Figure 8** shows, pressure has typically been high at a particular point, such as when the Philippine peso broke in early July 1997, and then it subsides. When pressure hits a high level, this measure does not indicate that the currency is about to devalue but rather that the currency is under a significant amount of pressure. Either confidence in the currency has to return or the central bank has to do something to change the sentiment; otherwise, the currency will devalue. At this point, the intelligence and market information become important. This measure is not sufficient by itself to determine whether a currency will be devalued, but for a layperson who does not continuously look at foreign exchange markets, this measure high-

Figure 6. History of Break-Even Standard Deviation for Thailand, September 1994–August 1997

Figure 7. Indicator of Currency Pressure: Asian Emerging Markets, April 9, 1997, through September 12, 1997

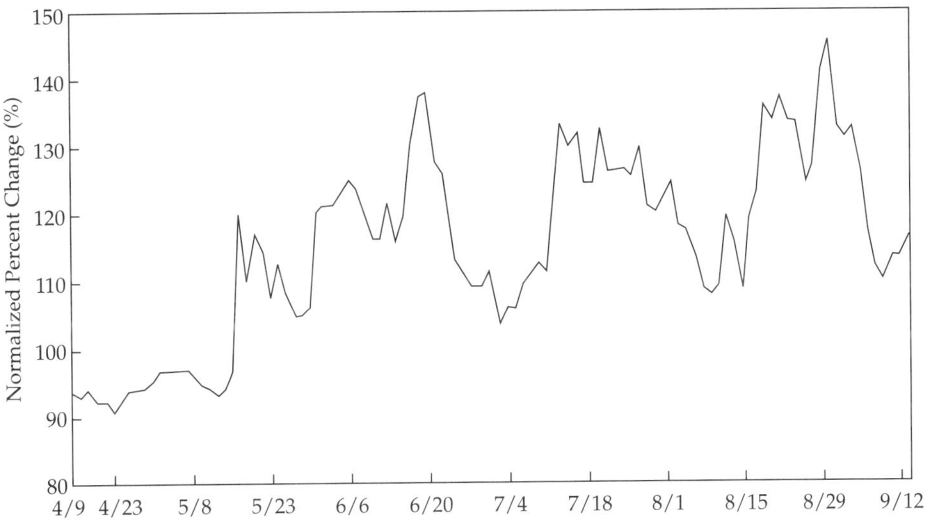

Note: Normalized percent change is measured in the domestic equity market over the prior two-week period.

Figure 8. Country-Specific Currency Pressure, April 9, 1997, through September 16, 1997

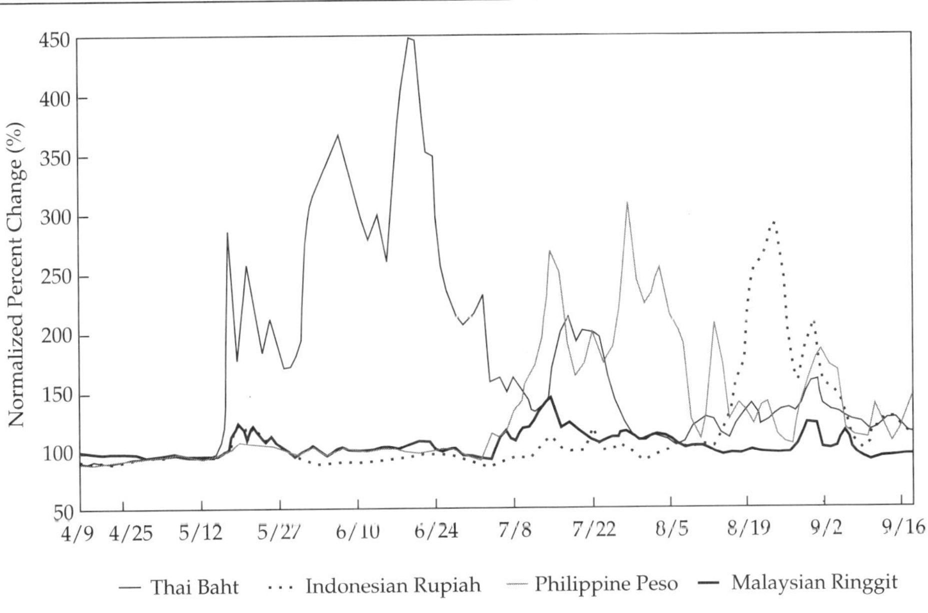

Note: Normalized percent change is measured in the domestic equity market over the prior two-week period.

lights which markets are under pressure at any point in time.

Foreign Exchange Regime Shifts. As pressure builds on a currency, investors often wonder whether a country's economic fundamentals indicate a potential currency devaluation. I will illustrate a type of model that helps focus on whether the economy is deteriorating in such a way that it indicates a likely shift in the way the currency is managed, which could mean a 10 percent devaluation or more. The approach is a simple one. We examined historical data on a large number of markets, emerging and developed—such as Australia and Canada. We tried to fit a model that is the best predictor of 10 percent or higher moves in currency. As with the two previous models I discussed, this model is not meant to be used in isolation to make currency decisions. This model should be blended with political risk assessments, economic outlooks, market positions, and fundamental analysis to estimate likely trends. This model is designed to add a quantitative input into currency forecasting.

We found that four fundamental economic variables have the most significance in terms of looking at currencies.

- *Currency defendability.* We use the ratio of the foreign exchange reserves of the country to money supply. M1 is the most quickly available money supply figure in most countries, so we use that for availability as opposed to M2. The higher (lower) the ratio of foreign exchange reserves to M1, the more (less) favorable the outlook for the currency.
- *Change in foreign exchange reserves.* We also measure the change in foreign exchange reserves, or more explicitly, how much the foreign exchange reserves have changed (as a percentage) over the past three months. An increase (decrease) in foreign exchange reserves over the previous quarter indicates a more (less) favorable outlook for the currency.
- *Market attractiveness.* Attractiveness of the market to other people is measured essentially by real interest rates. If real interest rates increase, then money tends to flow into the country. High real interest rates, however, can often be a panic measure, so this variable can be conflicting. On average, historically high interest rates tend to be favorable for currency and tend to attract money.
- *Real effective exchange rate differential.* The difference between the current real effective exchange rate (REER) and the five-year moving average is probably the most significant variable. The REER is a measure of the absolute strength of a currency and takes into account a country's inflation differentials compared with its trading partners. REER is essentially the best approximation of the fair value of a currency. It is fair value in the sense of export competitiveness, not in a purchasing power parity sense. The greater the upward deviation of REER from the five-year moving average, the less favorable the outlook for the currency.

The variables in this model indicate the overall likelihood of a currency devaluation. For example, **Figure 9** shows the model output for the probability of the Thai baht devaluating for the past five years. The probability was around 1 percent for most of the sample period. Then in May 1997, the probability of devaluation increased dramatically to almost 6 percent. This model provides a mathematical way of blending different economic information to come up with a feeling for whether a currency may devaluate.

Interest Rates. Interest rates in particular markets generally reflect the cost of hedging. Investors certainly want to know whether the current cost of hedging is high or low and if it is likely to increase. Although nominal interest rates provide some historical context, a look at real yields, measured by nominal rates less the latest consumer price index (CPI) figures, shows a different picture. To forecast interest rates, we try to figure out how the economy is likely to be viewed in a year's time. If it will be perceived by foreigners as being very risky, then one would expect to see high real interest rates. We try to determine an appropriate level for real interest rates, estimate our inflation forecasts, and blend the two together to derive our forecast of nominal interest rates.

Figure 9. Probability of Thai Baht Devaluation, June 1992–June 1997

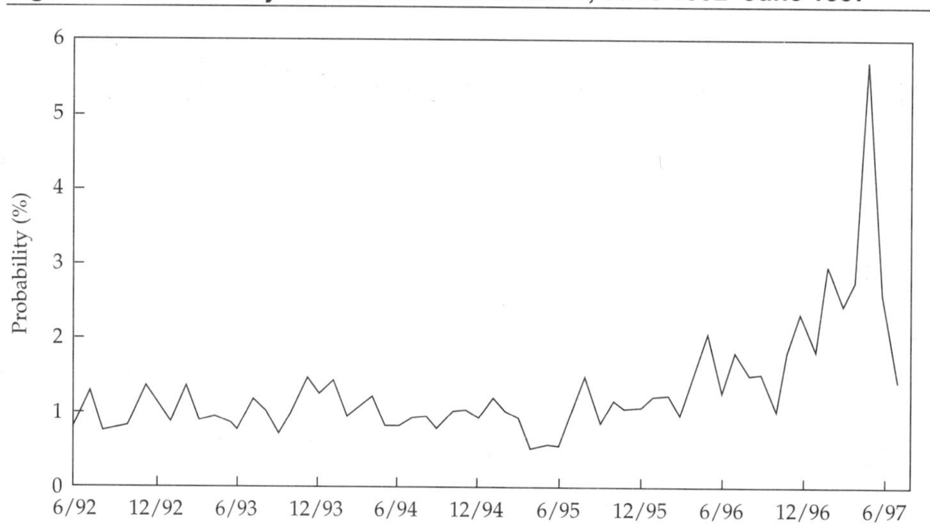

Nominal three-month interest rates in the Philippines during the past 10 years have ranged between 10 percent and 30 percent, but such a wide band does not help investors assess potential hedging costs. Nominal yields are not mean reverting but depend primarily on inflationary expectations. As **Figure 10** illustrates, real three-month interest rates exhibit mean reversion within a reasonable band. Traders like this type of pattern because when real rates move out of this band, they usually come back within the band. The wide 15 percent range on Figure 10 later dropped to about a 5 percent range in October 1997, which is a much more meaningful range. We conclude from this figure that real interest rates appear to be mean reverting; the 4–8 percent range shown in Figure 10 is a typical range for emerging markets, such as Thailand, and even for G–7 markets.

Thailand and the Philippines had very low rates during the 1988–96 period. Inflows of foreign capital, which have aided the liquidity and surplus in those markets, have probably been one of the major causes of the current currency weakness.

REER provides useful information on exchange rates, in particular, for determining fair value. The majority of countries maintain a REER between 85 percent and 115 percent of their five-year moving average. **Figure 11**, which shows the REER for a number of countries during the 1989–97 period, illustrates the impact of recent volatility on REER. For example, the Indonesian rupiah, Korean won, Malaysian ringgit, Hong Kong dollar, and Thai baht have all moved outside of this band. When real effective exchange rates break out of that 85–115 range, on either the upside or the downside, they tend to move back relatively quickly. So, 85–115 percent is a reasonable range for the fair value of a currency.

REER helps determine the value of a currency today. But for looking forward a year, a more dynamic equation is needed. One must consider how discounted the currency should be. Because REER takes inflation differentials into account, a currency has two ways to move back up. For example, as of October 27, 1997, Thailand had a REER of roughly 80 percent. Thailand's REER could move up to 85 percent by either having an instantaneous 5 percent strengthening against the dollar, or in practice against its trading partners, or it could stay where it is and have a 5 percent inflation differential over the next 12 months. Forecasting a currency's fair value is a dynamic process, but this general approach can be used to estimate where a currency's fair value might be headed by thinking of it as a discount to some range of fair value.

After the yen/dollar foreign exchange rate hit 80 in May 1995, many currencies gained in competitiveness because they were linked to the dollar, which strengthened over the following months. In particular, a strong yen/weak dollar improved the competitiveness of Asian markets. When the dollar turned around and started strengthening, the Thai baht in turn lost competitiveness. Because of the inflation picture and the situation with Thailand's other trading partners, the Thai baht REER went from about 93 percent up to 113 percent as shown in **Figure 12**, which is a 20 percent increase in valuation. This increase in valuation did not help the domestic system, and with foreign money also flowing into Thailand, the problems began.

We apply three factors to a forecast in what we call an "FVF" approach. The first "F" is for fundamentals. We look at the underlying economy and see what is likely to happen during the next three months and at how those fundamental changes will likely affect the market and the currency. The "V" is for valuation. We look at a country's REER to determine an appropriate valuation for that currency and how discounted it should be, given our knowledge of

Figure 10. Philippine Three-Month Real Interest Rates, 1988–97

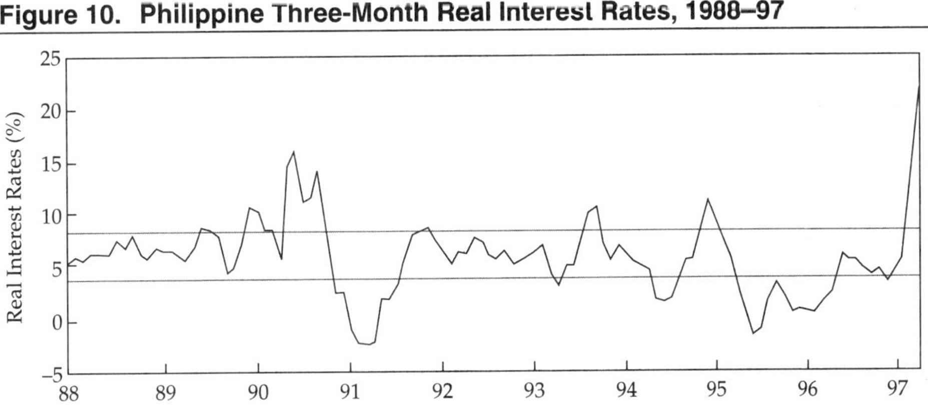

Figure 11. REER for Various Countries, December 1989–December 1997

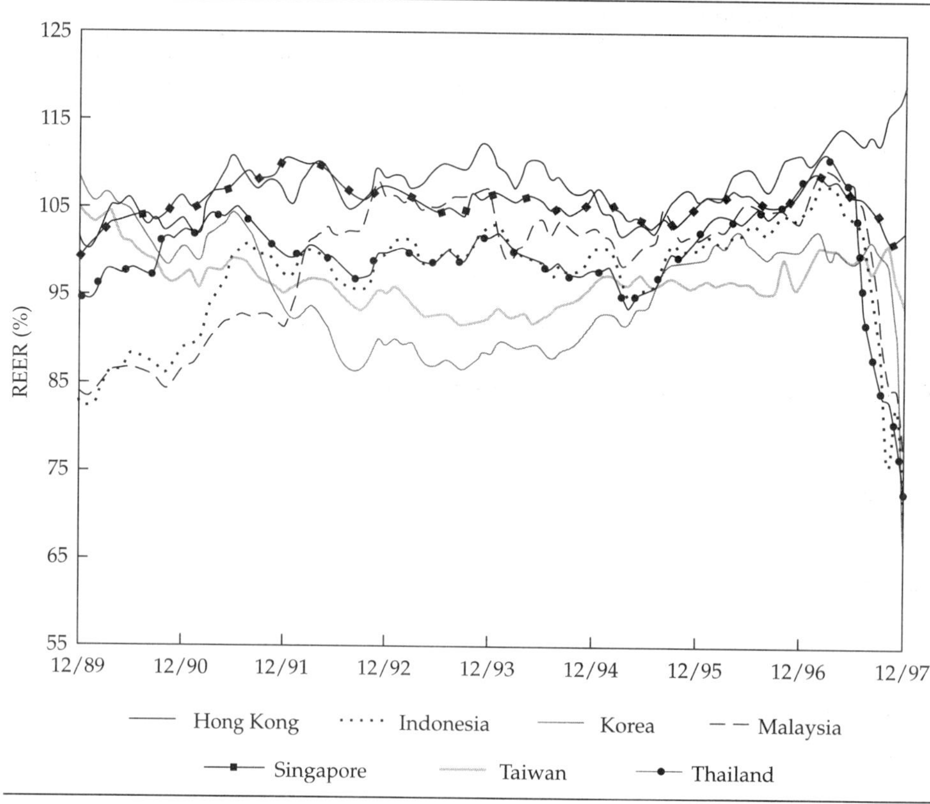

Figure 12. Thai Baht REER, May 1988–May 1997

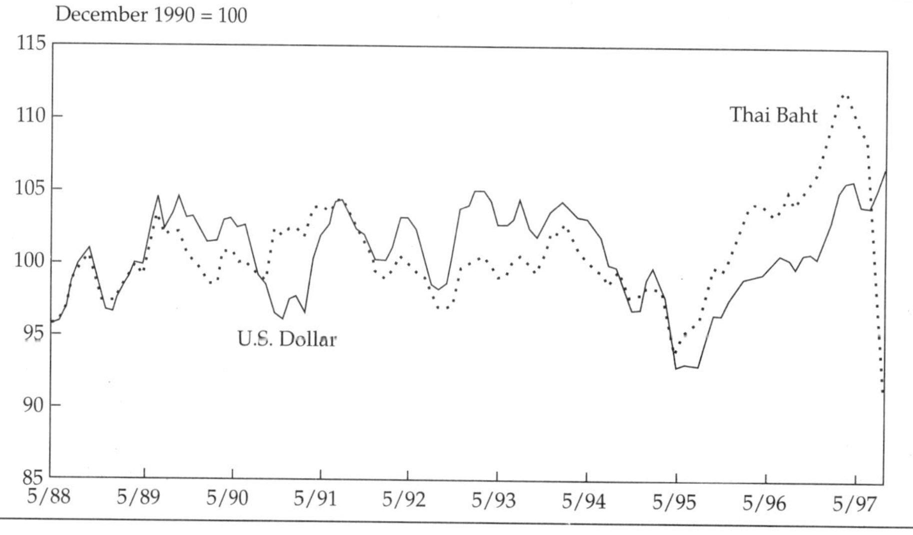

where the fundamentals tell us it is moving. The final "F" is an estimate of flows, which is probably the most important factor. We try to anticipate what the money flows through any currency will be. Throughout most of 1997, money flows have had a greater impact on Asian currency markets than on valuations. The fundamentals have certainly played a significant part, but at the end of the day, money flows have caused the currencies to move sharply.

Because so much volatility exists in the currency markets at any moment, a forecast will only provide a story and will never be totally correct. For example, **Table 4** provides our forecasts for various exchange rates as of September 15, 1997. We start with a particular date and then try to estimate where an exchange rate will move relative to the five-year REER. Our forecasts, again as of September 15, 1997, for interest rates are shown in **Table 5**. To estimate inflation, we

Table 4. Exchange Rate Forecasts for Various Currencies as of September 15, 1997

Period	Indonesian Rupiah	Malaysian Ringgit	Philippine Peso	Singapore Dollar	Thai Baht
Actual values					
End 1996	2,363	2.53	26.30	1.40	25.63
September 1997	2,938	2.95	32.20	1.51	35.05
Versus five-year REER	96%	99%	103%	105%	87%
Forecasted values					
End 1997	3,000	3.00	32.50	1.53	38
End 1998	3,100	3.20	30.00	1.50	42

Table 5. Offshore Interest Rate Forecasts for Various Currencies as of September 15, 1997

Forecast	Indonesian Rupiah	Malaysian Ringgit	Philippine Peso	Singapore Dollar	Thai Baht
Real rates					
1994–96 average	5.09%	3.00%[a]	4.10%	1.38%	3.44%
End 1997 estimate	7.00	5.80	6.00	2.00	9.00
End 1998 estimate	6.00	4.70	6.00	2.00	7.00
Inflation					
End 1997 CPI	9.0	3.2	10.0	2.5	9.0
End 1998 CPI	10.0	3.5	7.5	2.5	7.0
Three-month rates					
End 1997	16.0	9.0	16.0	4.5	18.0
End 1998	16.0	8.2	13.5	4.5	14.0

[a]Malaysia real rates averaged over 1995 and 1996.

Note: The offshore market is a nondeliverable forward market.

look at where real interest rates will likely go. Then we use real rates and inflation to build our forecasts of three-month interest rates. We have our historical range and our estimates as to where we would like to be in those ranges at particular dates.

Conclusion

The currency markets and the volatility of those markets have grown in importance, and therefore, currency hedging at certain times will be much more important for equity portfolios than it has been in the past. Currency movements significantly affect equity market returns. Some correlation exists between the two markets, but at times, the two markets will move very much out of line. Therefore, equity fund managers need to look at currency markets.

Evidence from the G–7 markets indicates that systematically hedging currency exposure using rolling currency hedges does not significantly reduce volatility in those markets. It is likely that the same holds true for Asian equity markets. Currency hedging must be much more tactical. A number of quantitative models are available to help make these currency-hedging decisions, but investors should also focus on market fundamentals, valuations, and capital flows.

Question and Answer Session

Michael C.M. Wilson

Question: Do you think the Hong Kong dollar will stay pegged to the U.S. dollar?

Wilson: This question has two answers: one for the short term and one for the long term. The Hong Kong dollar peg is fundamentally different from most other Asian countries' pegs. Other Asian markets could peg their currencies against either trade-weighted baskets or the U.S. dollar, but they have had no real mechanism in place to make that happen. Hong Kong has a mechanism whereby, in theory, every Hong Kong dollar has the backing of the currency reserve board with the essential link to the U.S. dollar. Therefore, with the Hong Kong reserves at US$88 billion and China's reserves at more than US$100 billion, Hong Kong has both the mechanism and ammunition to allow the peg to stay in place. So, the probability of the peg still being in place in the short term is fairly high.

In the long run, Hong Kong has no logical reason to link its currency to the U.S. dollar. Not a lot of synergy exists between the Hong Kong economy and the U.S. economy. If the strength of the U.S. dollar moves dramatically, it is logical that at some favorable point in the future that peg will be released. The Hong Kong authorities had enough ammunition to weather the recent storm, but they could pick some point in the reasonably distant future to release that peg.

An additional point to note is that most of Asia's economies are export-oriented, which makes the exchange rates relatively sensitive in terms of economic position. Hong Kong is a fundamentally different case. Manufacturing is approximately 7 percent of Hong Kong's economy. Hong Kong is essentially a service economy serving China. So, the pricing and the sensitivity of pricing is not as much through the exchange rate as the total cost of doing business.

Question: How are foreign exchange flows estimated?

Wilson: Foreign exchange flows can be looked at in several ways. Periodic snapshots are not quantitative, but every five years a survey is carried out that looks at the total trading flows in each financial center. I believe the last one was done in July or August 1996.

Another method depends on the nondeliverable markets. Some of those countries publish the amount of foreign exchange that is transacted each day. When looking at G–7 markets, you will find that four or five market players have a fairly dominant market share. J.P. Morgan is one of those players. Therefore, we can estimate with reasonable accuracy how much money flowed through the market in any particular day, and we can assume that we have a reasonably constant market share and that the actual number of trade tickets is high enough that it is unlikely to be very lumpy or have one big trade distort the estimate. Foreign exchange flows are not like stock markets, which have fixed turnover figures or open interest. Foreign exchange flows have to be estimated from market knowledge.

Question: What are the implications of currency hedging in Asia for non-U.S. investors?

Wilson: Currency hedging will essentially have the same relevance, regardless of the investor's base currency. My conclusion that systematic currency hedging is unlikely to reduce volatility also applies for hedging into yen or into any other Asian currency.

When we move into a more stable currency environment, I think we are likely to find that currencies behave to maintain their competitiveness. For example, up to early 1997, the Korean won and the new Taiwan dollar both had reasonable stability against a basket of currencies. They were not managed that way, but they were trying to stay competitive. Those baskets were essentially trade weighted. If we get back into regimes with volatility of 7 or 8 percent, we may find that those sorts of baskets provide more stability. In that case, it does affect your base currency.

If you are hedging into yen and you think there is a currency basket in play, you apply different types of currency hedges, and you can end up with different volatility measures. It depends on your base currency, and it depends on how the currency movements pan out as we go into 1998.

Question: Do you think the REER framework is inherently flawed in Asia because CPI measures do not adequately reflect inflationary pressures in terms of economic competitiveness and the real cost of capital?

Wilson: REER, which is more significant than real interest rates, has a number of flaws. The CPI measure is probably the worst in Malaysia, which uses a basket of currencies that consists of a significant number of government-fixed prices. When major sectors of the economy are left out from inflation calculations, then the result is certainly distorted.

In Singapore, REER does not account for increases in productivity. If Singapore has a structural change in the economy and productivity is continually improving, REER can keep going up without a loss in competitiveness. So, the question is, how good is REER as a proxy for competitiveness? The REER indicates what is happening to the trade picture or, in particular, the current account deficit. For each country, you can look at historical data to see how reliable or accurate it is, and then you need to modify your analysis in light of your findings. The relatively distorted inflation figures and the differences in productivity make REER a very difficult measure to use with confidence.

Question: If the key currency markets in Hong Kong, Indonesia, Malaysia, and Thailand are liquid, why do most large fund managers say they are too illiquid or expensive to use?

Wilson: In the currency markets, liquidity is relative and depends on the size of the position. In terms of the current markets, liquidity is low by historical standards. For Malaysia, Thailand, and Indonesia, we estimate the daily volume to be at least US$1.5 billion for forward contracts and about the same for spot contracts. So, liquidity depends on the size of the portfolio and the type of transaction you want to execute. If you are talking about a US$100 million or US$200 million hedging position, then I think the liquidity is available for hedging. But if you are trying to hedge a significantly larger equity portfolio, then you will run into problems. In terms of the spot foreign exchange, Malaysia, Thailand, and Indonesia are not markets where you can say liquidity will keep you from doing trades.

I would add that many people who use hedging do not hedge 100 percent. They use partial currency hedging, or they stagger their contracts over different days to overcome the size problem of wanting to hedge something on the order of US$1 billion.

Question: Why do you think the volatility of Asian currencies will settle at a lower rate than the U.S. dollar, yen, or German mark?

Wilson: I think the current situation is like a shock to the system and that the high volatility will dampen to an equilibrium band. I think these volatilities are likely to be low because most of these markets are relatively open. A lot of trading occurs within and between these countries. I think the trade flows mean that we are looking toward competitiveness and governments trying to maintain that competitiveness. These governments are not going to want extreme movements in their currencies. If you think of the trade as being roughly split into four equal parts held by Thailand, the United States, Asia, and Europe, then, when we get into a more stable situation, I think those high trade flows will mean lower volatility than the yen or the German mark, which are sentiment-driven currencies.

To come to this conclusion, I looked at the trade flows between Canada and the United States and the typical volatility of the Canadian dollar and the U.S. dollar. The trade flow between Canada and the United States is about 2–3 percent, which is low compared with other markets. The trade flow between the United States and Japan is at the high end of the spectrum, so I think that the volatility will probably settle in the higher of those two ranges. It may take two years to find out if my prediction is correct. High shocks and high instability could continue for some time. My prediction will also depend on the openness of information. If we continually get shocks from countries and are unaware of the total amount of problems in the finance sectors, then we will continually get new information that could cause big moves in the currencies.

Self-Evaluation Examination

1. According to Roche, which of the following can help resolve the currency crises in East Asia?
   I. Maintaining the Hong Kong dollar peg.
   II. Tightening fiscal policy to run a surplus and improve the current account.
   III. Reforming, regulating, and liberalizing the financial sector.
   IV. Decreasing the domestic content of infrastructure projects and exports.
   A. I and IV.
   B. II and III.
   C. I and IV.
   D. III and IV.

2. Roche suggests that East Asia has two crises: a crisis of excessive external deficits and a domestic capital crisis.
   A. True.
   B. False.

3. Roche claims that the overall impact of the East Asian crises will be higher risk premiums, higher interest rates, higher economic growth, and higher growth in profits.
   A. True.
   B. False.

4. Research on Asian equities can best be characterized by which of the following statements?
   I. As Asian markets mature, the level of difficulty and thoroughness of required research increases while the value added from the research decreases.
   II. Company visits are a valuable source of information and help identify problems.
   III. Understanding the industry paradigm in which industries operate is crucial.
   IV. Using the dividend discount model in Asian emerging markets is straightforward.
   A. I and IV.
   B. II and IV.
   C. I, II, and III.
   D. All of the above.

5. According to Zielinski, which of the following analytical techniques provide insight into Asian equity research?
   A. Event studies.
   B. Cluster analyses.
   C. Impact assessments.
   D. All of the above.

6. Structural, industrial, psychological, and informational asymmetries influence the relative performance of alternative equity styles.
   A. True.
   B. False.

7. When the ________ cycle peaks and starts to decelerate, ________ managers outperform ________ managers.
   A. interest rate, growth, value.
   B. profit, value, growth.
   C. interest rate, value, growth.
   D. profit, growth, value.

8. During periods of ________ interest rates, ________ funds outperform ________ funds.
   A. low or declining, value, growth.
   B. high or increasing, growth, value.
   C. low or declining, growth, value.
   D. stable, growth, value.

9. Growth and value strategies work in Asia.
   A. True.
   B. False.

10. Bernstein and Tupper think that tactical allocation, or market timing of styles, adds tremendous value.
    A. True.
    B. False.

11. According to Schwob, which of the following conditions is the most important in assessing the relevance of style factors?
    A. Consistency.
    B. Regularity.
    C. Attribution.
    D. Identity.

12. Which of the following statements most accurately reflects Schwob's opinion of style analysis in non-U.S. markets?
    A. Style is relevant, meaningful, and important in the vast majority of non-U.S. markets.
    B. Properly applied style analysis reveals details about the portfolio manager's investment orientation and philosophy.
    C. Sector adjustment neutralizes the effects of sector imbalances on style analysis.
    D. All of the above.

13. For Krueger to consider adding a company to his portfolio, it must have which of the following characteristics?
    A. The company must have fundamentals that can be analyzed.
    B. Long (short) positions must trade at a 20 percent discount (premium) to fair value.
    C. A catalyst must be present that will result in a revaluation of the stock.
    D. All of the above.

14. Which of the following approaches best addresses liquidity and diversification concerns in Asia ex-Japan?
    A. Static hedging.
    B. Limits based on a security's trading volume, free float, and country exposure.
    C. Limits on the number of markets in which the fund is invested.
    D. None of the above.

15. Systematic hedging is the best solution to reducing currency risk in Asian equity portfolios.
    A. True.
    B. False.

16. According to Wilson, which of the following factors has the strongest influence on the currency-hedging decision?
    A. Interest rate differentials.
    B. Equity market volatility.
    C. Economic growth measured by GNP.
    D. Government fiscal and monetary policy.

17. Which of the following, in Wilson's opinion, indicate a more favorable outlook for a nation's currency?
    I. A low ratio of foreign exchange reserves to M1.
    II. An increase in foreign exchange reserves over the previous quarter.
    III. A small upward deviation of the real effective exchange rate from the five-year moving average.
    IV. Low real interest rates relative to other countries.

    A. I and III.
    B. II and III.
    C. I, II, and IV.
    D. II and III.

Self-Evaluation Answers

1. B. Roche suggests that the cure for resolving the currency crises in East Asia is straightforward. The recipe for recovery includes floating currencies; keeping interest rates fairly high, but lower than needed to defend the currency itself; tightening fiscal policies to run a surplus and improve the current account; reforming, regulating, and liberalizing the financial sector; deregulating the economy to raise competitiveness; increasing the domestic content of infrastructure projects and exports; and raising and improving domestic research and development spending.

2. A. Low export growth coupled with an extremely high propensity to import and fast domestic demand growth have created exceptionally high external deficits in East Asia. East Asia's second major problem is capital overhang. At the peak of the U.S. economic cycle, when East Asia's exports were booming and the United States was running a big current account deficit, the world was flooded with dollars and East Asia got swamped with liquidity. East Asian banks had to keep interest rates low to prevent their currencies from appreciating under the pressure of the inflow of U.S. dollars. Low interest rates made capital cheap and plentiful, which led to increased investment in marginal and unproductive projects.

3. B. The overall impact of the East Asian crises will be higher risk premiums, higher interest rates, lower economic growth, and lower growth in profits.

4. C. Zielinski states that one of the difficulties of using the dividend discount model in Asian emerging markets is choosing an appropriate discount rate. Because no long-term government bond yields exist in Asian emerging markets for determining a risk-free rate of interest, he calculates a synthetic one based on U.S. rates, local interest rates, and the local inflation rate. The number of different economies and interest rates also makes using the DDM a challenge.

5. D. Event studies are useful for analyzing how a currency devaluation might affect profits in a certain industry, for example, banking. Cluster analyses can show how an industry might behave in different markets. Impact assessments help quantify the size of opportunities or problems.

6. B. According to Bernstein, structural, psychological, and informational asymmetries explain the relative performance of alternative equity styles. Structural segments of the market are created when managers (or their clients) restrict the investment universe. Psychological biases, such as regret aversion, also influence performance. All companies do not have the same information flow, which results in information asymmetries, for example, between large- and small-cap firms.

7. D. When the profit cycle peaks and starts to decelerate, growth managers outperform value managers. Bernstein explains that as earnings become scarce, investors bid up the price of that scarce resource and multiples expand on the companies that can maintain their growth rates.

8. C. Bernstein states that growth funds outperform value funds in periods of declining or low interest rates and that value outperforms growth in periods of rising or high interest rates. Growth stocks, which have longer durations than value stocks, tend to be more interest rate sensitive than value stocks.

9. A. Although growth and value strategies work in Asia, the success of these strategies depends on the market. Tupper shows that the Asia Pacific ex-Japan markets provide a good example of how a preferred style of investing varies by the country under consideration.

10. B. Bernstein and Tupper think that strategic allocation can add value but tactical allocation, with its reliance on correct timing and asset selection, is a waste of time. Too many decisions have to be made, and too many errors can result.

11. D. The most important condition for assessing the relevance of style factors is identity (i.e., stocks must cluster in distinct performance groupings).

12. D.

13. D. When fundamentals can be analyzed, when the valuations are attractive, and when identifiable catalysts are present, Krueger will consider adding the company to his portfolio.

14. B. Restricting the portfolio from owning more than 10 percent of any security's free float and more than 10 days of the average trading volume helps Krueger provide sufficient liquidity to meet fund redemptions. Investing in at least five countries throughout the region and limiting the maximum exposure in any one country to 35 percent ensures adequate portfolio diversification.

15. B. Wilson predicts that if Asian markets follow the route of most G–7 markets, systematic hedging of all currency exposure is unlikely to be a good solution and will not reduce volatility. He concludes that tactical hedging will be more appropriate.

16. A. When investors are trying to decide whether to hedge currency exposure, Wilson recommends that they think about currency volatility, interest rate differentials, currency trends, and event risk. If investors expect high short-term currency volatility, short-term currency depreciation, or the likelihood of a sharp currency devaluation, they will be more likely to hedge the currency. High interest rate differentials increase the cost of hedging and make investors less likely to hedge currency exposure.

17. D. The higher (lower) the ratio of foreign exchange reserves to M1, the more (less) favorable the outlook for the currency. An increase (decrease) in foreign exchange reserves over the previous quarter indicates a more (less) favorable outlook for the currency. The greater the upward deviation of the real effective exchange rate from the five-year moving average, the less favorable the outlook for the currency. High real interest rates historically attract money flows into a country, but they can often be a panic measure.

Selected Publications

AIMR

AIMR Performance Presentation Standards Handbook, 2nd edition, 1997

Deregulation of the Electric Utility Industry, 1997

Economic Analysis for Investment Professionals, 1997

Finding Reality in Reported Earnings, 1997
Jan R. Squires, CFA, *Editor*

Global Bond Management, 1997
Jan R. Squires, CFA, *Editor*

Implementing Global Equity Strategy: Spotlight on Asia, 1997

Investing in Small-Cap and Microcap Securities, 1997

Investing Worldwide VIII: Developments in Global Portfolio Management, 1997

Managing Currency Risk, 1997

Standards of Practice Casebook, 1996

Standards of Practice Handbook, 7th edition, 1996

Research Foundation

Blockholdings of Investment Professionals
by Sanjai Bhagat, Bernard S. Black, and Margaret M. Blair

Company Performance and Measures of Value Added
by Pamela P. Peterson, CFA, and David R. Peterson

Controlling Misfit Risk in Multiple-Manager Investment Programs
by Jeffery V. Bailey, CFA, and David E. Tierney

Country Risk in Global Financial Management
by Claude B. Erb, CFA, Campbell R. Harvey, and Tadas E. Viskanta

Economic Foundations of Capital Market Returns
by Brian D. Singer, CFA, and Kevin Terhaar, CFA

Initial Dividends and Implications for Investors
by James W. Wansley, CFA, William R. Lane, CFA, and Phillip R. Daves

Interest Rate Modeling and the Risk Premiums in Interest Rate Swaps
Robert Brooks, CFA

Sales-Driven Franchise Value
Martin L. Leibowitz

U.S. POSTAL SERVICE
STATEMENT OF OWNERSHIP, MANAGEMENT, AND CIRCULATION
(Required by 39 U.S.C. 3685)

1. Title of Publication: *ICFA Continuing Education*
2. Publication No.:
3. Filing Date: January 19, 1998
4. Issue Frequency: Seven Times a Year
5. Number of Issues Published Annually: 7
6. Annual Subscription Price: US$100
7. Complete Mailing Address of Known Office of Publication (Street, City, County, State, and Zip+4) (Not Printer)
   Association for Investment Management and Research
   P.O. Box 3668, Charlottesville, VA 22903-0668
8. Complete Mailing Address of Headquarters or General Business Office of Publisher (Not Printer)
   Association for Investment Management and Research
   P.O. Box 3668, Charlottesville, VA 22903-0668
9. Full Names and Complete Mailing Addresses of Publisher, Editor, and Managing Editor (Do Not Leave Blank)
   Publisher (Name and Complete Mailing Address)
   Jaynee M. Dudley, AIMR, P.O. Box 3668, Charlottesville, VA 22903-0668
   Editor (Name and Complete Mailing Address)
   Katrina F. Sherrerd, AIMR, P.O. Box 3668, Charlottesville, VA 22903-0668
   Managing Editor (Name and Complete Mailing Address)
   Bette Collins, AIMR, P.O. Box 3668, Charlottesville, VA 22903-0688
10. Owner (If owned by a corporation, its name and address must be stated and also immediately thereafter the names and addresses of stockholders owning or holding 1 percent or more of the total amount of stock. If not owned by a corporation, the names and addresses of the individual owners must be given. If owned by a partnership or other unincorporated firm, its name and address as well as that of each individual must be given. If the publication is published by a nonprofit organization, its name and address must be given.) (Do Not Leave Blank)
    Association for Investment Management and Research, P.O. Box 3668,
    Charlottesville, VA 22903-0668
11. Known Bondholders, Mortgagees, and Other Security Holders Owning or Holding 1 Percent or More of Total Amount of Bonds, Mortgages or Other Securities. If none, check here. ✔ None.
12. For completion by nonprofit organization authorized to mail at special rates. The purpose, function, and nonprofit status of the organization and the exempt status for Federal income tax purposes: (Check one.)

    ✔ Has Not Changed During Preceding 12 Months

    Has Changed During Preceding 12 Months (If changed, publisher must submit explanation of change with this statement.)
13. Publication Name: *Financial Analysts Jounal*
14. Issue Date for Circulation Data Below: January/February 1997 through November/December 1997

15. Extent and Nature of Circulation	Average No. Copies Each Issue During Preceding 12 Months	Actual No. of Copies of Single Issue Published Nearest to Filing Date
a. Total No. Copies (Net Press Run)	24,010	23,140
b. Paid and/or Requested Circulation		
1. Sales Through Dealers and Carriers, Street Vendors, and Counter Sales		
2. Paid or Requested Mail Subscriptions	22,363	25,255
c. Total Paid and/or Requested Circulation (sum of 15b(1) and 15b(2))	22,363	25,255
d. Free Distribution by Mail, Samples, Complimentary, and Other Free	203	200
e. Free Distribution Outside the Mail		
f. Total Distribution (sum of 15d and 15e)	203	200
g. Total Distribution (sum of 15c and 15f)	22,565	25,455
h. Copies Not Distributed		
1. Office Use, Leftovers, Spoiled	2,665	2,350
2. Returns from News Agents		
i. Total (sum of 15g, 15h(1), and 15h(2))	25,231	27,805
Percent Paid and/or Requested Circulation (15c/15g × 100)	100	100

16. This Statement of Ownership will be printed in the 1998, vol. 1, no. 1 issue of this publication.
17. I certify that all information furnished on this form is true and complete. I understand that anyone who furnishes false or misleading information on this form or who omits material or information requested on the form may be subject to criminal sanctions (including fines and imprisonment) and/or civil sanctions (including multiple damages and civil penalties).

Signature and Title of Editor, Publisher, Business Manager, or Owner
Jaynee Dudley, Publisher